IMAGES
of America

HISTORIC
GRANT PARK

This current photograph of Lemuel Pratt Grant's mansion, built in 1857, provides a glimpse into a piece of the neighborhood's past and what could have been its future. The home is now the headquarters of the Atlanta Preservation Center where efforts are underway to restore the structure to its original three stories. Author proceeds from the purchase of this book are dedicated to these efforts, and it is hoped that these pages will encourage others to assist in similar fashion. (Courtesy Atlanta Preservation Center.)

ON THE COVER: A six-acre, man-made lake captured the waters of numerous natural springs in and around Grant Park. The long, shallow lake came to be named Abana after a river outside of Damascus, Syria. Referenced in the Bible in 2 Kings 5:12: "Are not Abana and Pharpar, rivers of Damascus, better than all the rivers of Israel?" The name Abana means "gathering of waters." The lake was the focal point of Atlanta's new park and was recognized as "its most important asset" by John Charles Olmsted of the famed Olmsted Brothers landscape design firm. (Courtesy Kenan Research Center at the Atlanta History Center.)

IMAGES
of America

HISTORIC
GRANT PARK

Jennifer Goad Cuthbertson and
Philip M. Cuthbertson

ARCADIA
PUBLISHING

Published by Arcadia Publishing
Charleston, South Carolina

Library of Congress Control Number: 2010937084

For all general information, please contact Arcadia Publishing:
Telephone 843-853-2070
Fax 843-853-0044
E-mail sales@arcadiapublishing.com
For customer service and orders:
Toll-Free 1-888-313-2665

Visit us on the Internet at www.arcadiapublishing.com

*For everyone who sees the treasures of Atlanta, and the
state of Georgia, and seeks to preserve them forever.*

CONTENTS

ACKNOWLEDGMENTS

There are many individuals and institutions that deserve recognition for their contributions to this endeavor. Thanks goes to the following: Phillip Northman, Robin South, Mike and Carolyn Dufano, Lorna Gentry, Rick Jones, Jeff McCord, and Bob Ward, who generously gave their time, their knowledge, their maps, postcards, and photographs, as well as the Park Avenue Baptist Church and St. Paul United Methodist Church for opening up their libraries to us. There are also several past and present residents David and Marian Dye, Charles Chosewood, and Jeanne Shorthouse who each offered the same. A sincere thank you is extended to all.

Atlanta is fortunate to have several institutions who actively work to preserve the rich heritage of this city. The Atlanta Preservation Center has purchased the original Grant Mansion and is slowly restoring it to its former splendor and has worked to document the history and the architecture of not only Grant Park, but the city as a whole. The Atlanta History Center has a rich archive full of photographs and materials documenting the birth and growth of Atlanta. The Georgia Archives Vanishing Georgia Collection has a rich treasure trove of photographs, as does Georgia State University. All of these institutions have been very generous in opening up their resources to us.

We also wish to thank the residents of this neighborhood for being so passionate about it and the houses and park that comprise it. Thanks to those who recognized its character and charm and dared to remain or move here during the 1970s and 1980s to begin restoring, renovating, and rebuilding the homes and businesses here.

We are very appreciative of Arcadia Publishing who understands the importance of the history—with special thanks to our editor, Brinkley Taliaferro, who helped guide us through the home stretch of this project. Through their books and publications, they are working to preserve the past for future generations.

To our families, friends, and colleagues who have listened to us discuss the book and who have provided support and encouragement, thank you.

INTRODUCTION

Unto each man his handiwork, unto each his crown the just fate gives
Whoso takes the world's life on him and his own lays down, He, dying so, lives.

—From the poem by Charles Algernon Swinburne,
read at the 1910 unveiling of a monument for Col. Lemuel P. Grant,
the man behind the park and the neighborhood

Atlanta is a town whose fortunes were founded on the railroad. It was a hub for rail activity in the Southeast during the 1800s, and Lemuel Pratt Grant was one of the men at the forefront of the railroad industry. Born in August 1817, Grant was a product of Frankfurt, Maine. He was a self-taught civil engineer, and his ambition went well beyond the boundaries of his family farm. By becoming a rodman for the engineering corps of the Philadelphia & Reading Railroad, he wrote his ticket off the farm and into a prominent role as railroad scion, military man, and philanthropist in Atlanta, Georgia.

In January 1840, Grant accepted an offer as assistant engineer in the engineer corps of the Georgia Railroad and moved to Atlanta, then known as Marthasville. Grant worked his way up the ranks through various railroad companies. Along the way, he accumulated a vast wealth, and in 1846, a portion of his income was used to purchase 600-plus acres of land, some for 75¢ an acre and the rest for $2 an acre.

Lemuel P. Grant became a colonel in the Confederate army in 1862 and, as the chief engineer for the Department of Militia, he was commissioned to repair and reconstruct Georgia railways damaged by federal troops. He was also charged with designing defensive fortifications for the city of Atlanta.

Besides being a railroad man, a member of the military, and a philanthropist, Col. Lemuel P. Grant was also a great reader, preferring the works of Charles Dickens, and he is reported to have owned both the first piano and the first carriage brought to Atlanta. The colonel built an antebellum, brick-and-stucco mansion for his family and loved to walk through the woods on his property and enjoy the natural springs and abundant bird life. He opted to share this bounty with the citizens of Atlanta.

In 1883, he donated 100 acres of land to the city to create a public park. The deed for the city's oldest park proclaims the following: "To have and to hold said tract of land, as part and parcel of the L.P. Grant Park to the use of said City of Atlanta forever, on condition that the same shall be maintained by said City as a public park, and shall not be used for any purpose inconsistent with its use as a public park, and that spirituous liquors shall not be sold thereon."

Sydney Root, a close friend of Grant, was appointed the first park commissioner of the city and charged with supervising the construction of the park. The city initially spent $3,500 on materials and labor to turn Colonel Grant's gift into a park. In the mid-1880s, discussions began with the Frederick Law Olmsted design firm, designer of New York's Central Park, to develop the new park. However, the firm was not formally under contract until 1903, and by that time Frederick had died, so John Charles Olmsted, Frederick's stepson, took on the commission and worked to make Colonel Grant's vision for a serene, pastoral space a reality.

The original design of the park featured many winding, shaded pathways named after Georgia's major cities and incorporated the natural springs that Colonel Grant so loved.

In 1885, then Atlanta mayor George Hillyer said, "A place of recreation like this is of inestimable value to our hard-working citizens and industrious population. Nothing promotes more, both the moral and mental, as well as physical health, than such a place of resort and recreation."

The 430 acres of the Grant Park residential neighborhood got its start in the 1880s when Colonel Grant began subdividing and selling his land, as did property owners living in close proximity to the new park. Deeds indicate that the street pattern was in place by 1883. By the time of Grant's death in 1893, many of the lots were already sold.

Efforts were also undertaken to connect the newly developed neighborhood with the city of Atlanta. In 1883, the Metropolitan Street Railway Company established a streetcar service with four separate lines traveling to the area, and for the cost of 10¢ a ride, anyone could travel to the "people's playground," as Grant Park came to be known. In May 1887, the city began work on a series of boulevards connecting Grant Park to Peachtree Street, Georgia and Capitol Avenues, Washington and Pryor Streets, and West End.

Grant Park also became home to other amenities that still bring pleasure to tourists and city residents alike. In 1889, as the park and neighborhood were taking shape, George Gress purchased a defunct traveling circus at an auction on the steps of the Fulton County Courthouse. His ultimate goal was to acquire the wagons and railroad cars that were part of the circus, and Gress offered the animals to the city of Atlanta.

A collection of one hyena, two African lionesses, two silver lions, one black bear, two wildcats, one jaguar, one gazelle, one raccoon, one elk, one Mexican hog, two deer, one camel, one dromedary, two monkeys, and two serpents made up the first zoo in the city. Gress erected housing and cages for the animals in Grant Park. The Grant Park Zoo opened in April 1889. Gress is also responsible for bringing the *Atlanta Cyclorama*, an 18,000-pound, 50-foot-high painting of the Atlanta campaign of 1864, to Grant Park.

The Grant Park neighborhood reached its zenith in the early 1900s and prospered until its war with the automobile began. The first battle in the early 1900s siphoned off wealthier residents who could now afford cars and were drawn to neighborhoods that were farther away from the city. They began to move to the wealthier suburbs of Druid Hills, Morningside, and Buckhead. Despite this, Grant Park remained an upper-middle-class neighborhood into the 1950s.

The 1960s marked the second battle with the automobile and was the period when the automobile did the most damage to the neighborhood. In the name of progress, Grant Park was cut in half with the construction of a four-lane highway, Interstate 20. Interstate 20 severely disrupted the neighborhood and caused it to decline in the wake of its construction. Many homes were divided into multifamily units and owner-occupied homes were harder and harder to find. Crime rose, and at its lowest point, Grant Park was labeled one of the highest crime areas in Atlanta.

Recognizing the potential in the fading beauty of Victorian-era homes that they found, a few urban pioneers moved to the neighborhood in the 1970s and began to restore the decaying treasures. The 1980s and 1990s saw the neighborhood blossom again, and as people seek to live closer to their jobs and the amenities of the city, the neighborhood continues to flourish. Demolition of older homes has largely been halted, and the entire area was placed on the National Register of Historic Places in 1979, which paved the way for the neighborhood to receive historic designation by the City of Atlanta, ensuring that the character of the neighborhood will remain intact.

One

A GIFT TO THE CITY

For "the public good," the deed to Grant Park was formally executed on May 17, 1883, with a stipulation that the land should always be used for park purposes; a violation of this would result in the forfeiture of the title.

In an address delivered in 1910 at a ceremony unveiling a monument in the park to Colonel Grant, the speaker talked about Grant's motivation for the donation: "So, he gave this park that the city might not be all man-made, and its people not be left entirely to themselves; but that the children might have a place to play and the weary laden toilers an opportunity for the rest and peace which sometimes can come only under waving trees in the silent woods."

Colonel Grant's gift of land, and the foresight to designate it for a park, has given the city its oldest park, which was, and still is, an urban oasis. The vision of John Charles Olmsted led to the majority of Grant Park being left in a pastoral state with great lawns and fields of grass. The book *The Gate City: Atlanta*, published in 1890, describes one as "a magnolia lawn, which makes a brilliant patch of color in the park, with its beds of scarlet salvia, dusty miller, colias, gentian bloomers and ageratum, which blend in a harmony of blue and red and silver."

In the early days, Lake Abana was one of the dominant features, drawing people from all over to walk around its periphery. A boathouse sheltered canoes that visitors could rent for a minimal sum and row across the lake. In the center of the lake was a small island built of rock and sand that was landscaped with plants that bloomed beautifully in the summer. Then, and now, this generous gift of land to the citizens of Atlanta has provided many happy returns to those visiting and living near it.

An early business and civic leader and philanthropist, Lemuel Pratt Grant (1817–1893) moved to the small settlement of Marthasville, Georgia, in 1840 to work as an assistant in the engineer corps for the Georgia Railroad. His work placed him at the forefront of rail expansion and growth in an ambitious town. New rail lines provided connections for commerce and industry, and the town began to grow. In his book, *Atlanta and Its Environs*, historian Franklin Garrett refers to Grant as "the Father of Atlanta." Grant was involved in a number of civic activities, such as establishing a public school system in the city (1868), raising funds to move Oglethorpe University to Atlanta from Milledgeville (1870), participating as a board member for the Bank of the State of Georgia, and belonging to city council. (Courtesy Kenan Research Center at the Atlanta History Center.)

Atlanta, Ga, Grant Park.

The land that would become L.P. Grant Park was a popular destination for city dwellers long before its official designation as a public space. To escape the dirt, soot, and noise of town, visitors came to enjoy the shade of its trees, the cool waters of its natural springs, and the quiet of its riding and walking trails. While not the first park in the city, it was certainly the largest and most visited. It was not long before its benefits to a growing city were recognized and other land was set aside for similar purpose. Many of the original features are gone, public art has vanished, and the grounds are a bit threadbare. But it survives today as the oldest of Atlanta's existing public parks and continues to be one of the most visited. (Courtesy Phillip Northman Collection.)

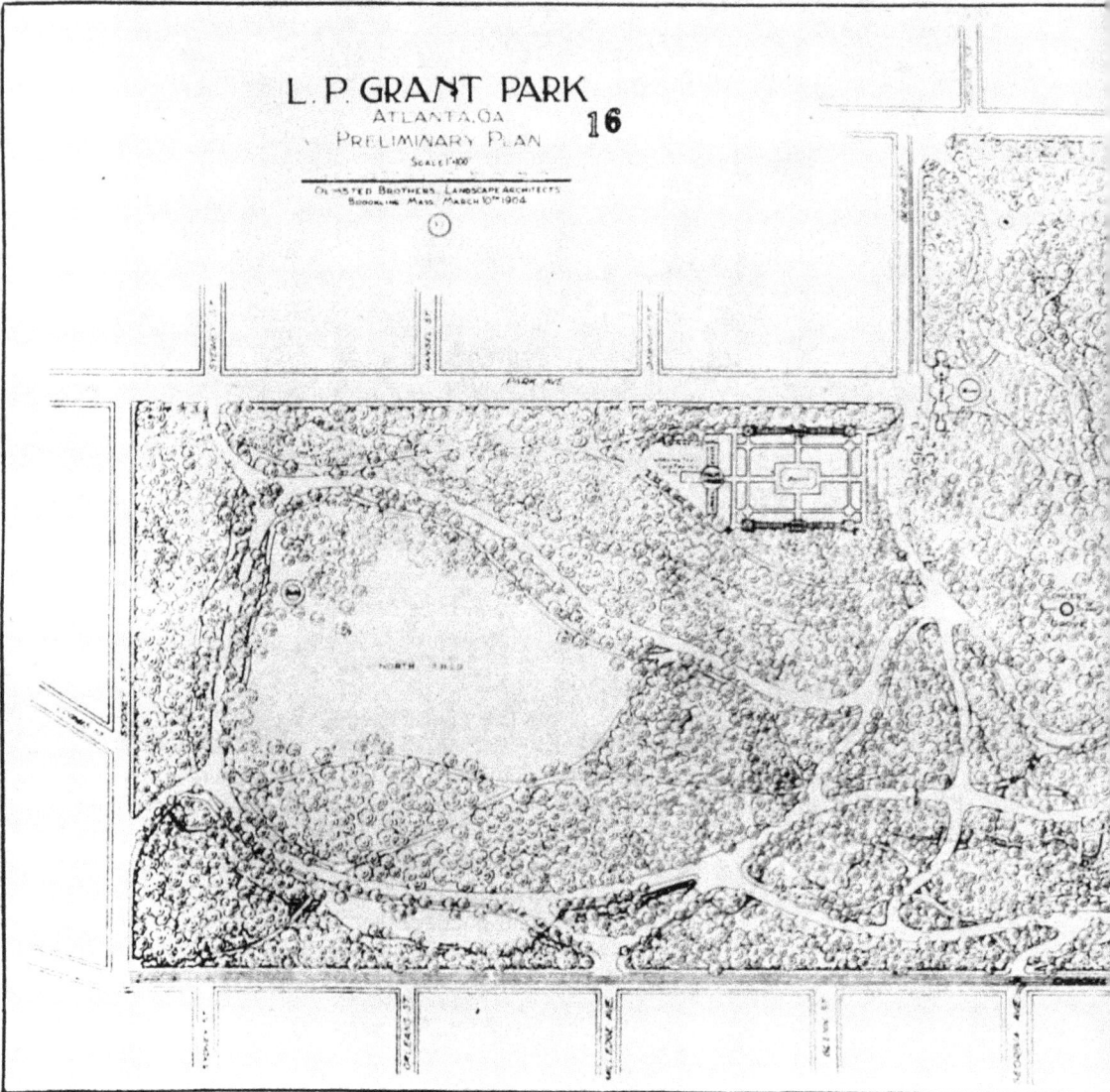

L. P. GRANT PARK
ATLANTA, GA
PRELIMINARY PLAN
SCALE 1"=100'

OLMSTED BROTHERS, LANDSCAPE ARCHITECTS
BROOKLINE, MASS. MARCH 10TH 1904

16

After years of discussion and 21 years after Col. Lemuel P. Grant deeded the land for the park to the city, the Park Commission contracted with the Olmsted Brothers design firm to create a development plan for Grant Park. This 1904 map was part of the plan submitted. It recognizes and includes existing features, such as walkways, carriageways, Lake Abana, Fort Walker, the

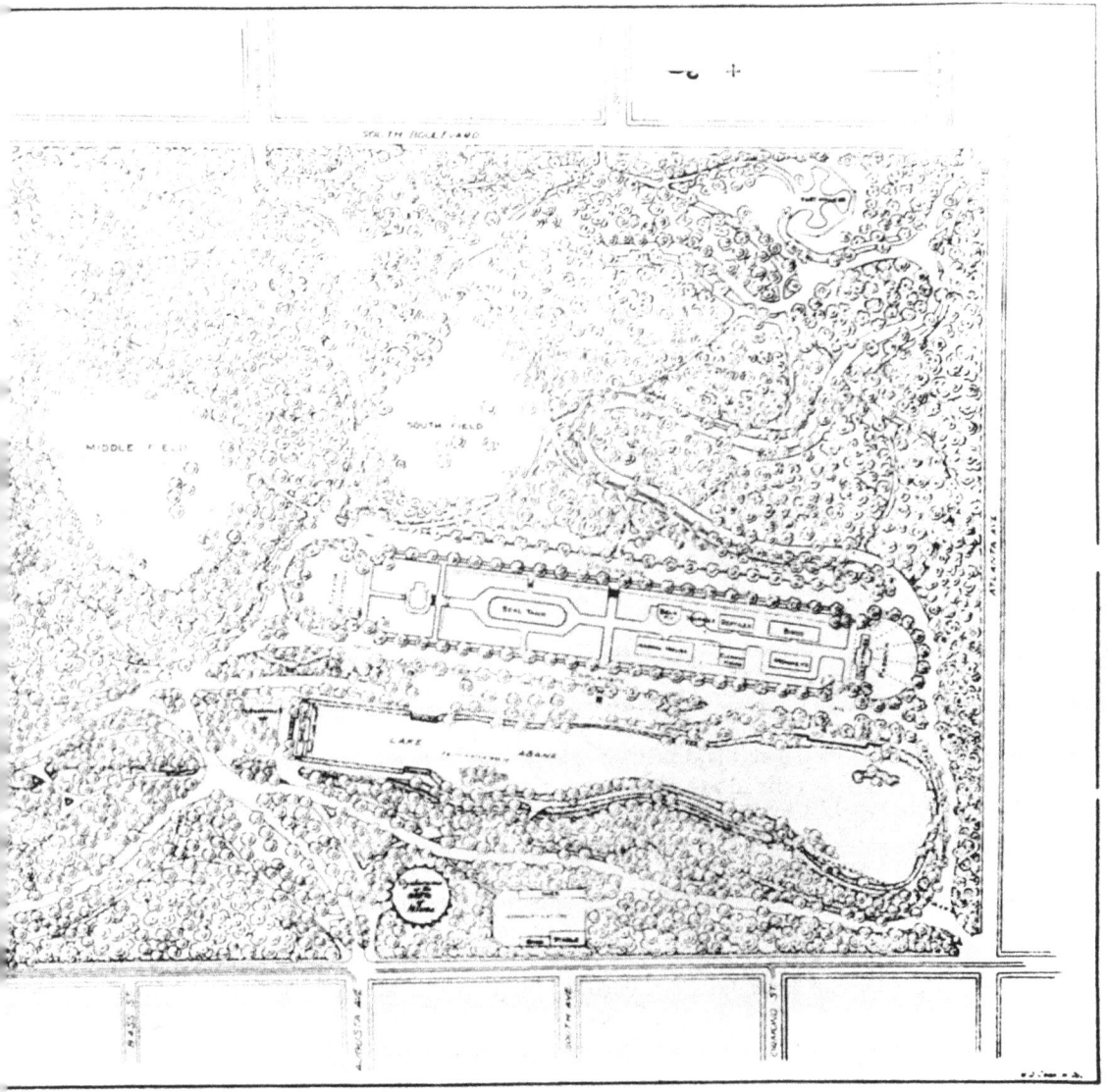

zoo, and the cyclorama. Recognizing the need for additional space for more active recreation, the plan also included a South Field, Middle Field, and North Field and called for a small pond in the northwest section of the park. (Courtesy CRAFT, LLC.)

Scene in Grant Park, showing Grant Monument,
Atlanta, Ga.

The monument depicted in this December 1918 postcard was placed in the park to honor Lemuel Grant for his gift and the many other civic engagements undertaken in his lifetime. At the dedication in June 1910, Joseph C. Logan said, "Colonel Grant had the gift of this park in mind years before he made it. We of his family know that he held deep community with nature, and had the love of it in his heart. We know that he walked through these woods, and saw its springs bubbling over with clear water, and heard the catbird and the robin and the blue jay and the thrush overflowing in song with pure joy of living, that he foresaw the time when human habitations would dry up the springs and rob the birds of their nests and trees." The monument was removed in 1917 with plans for a new honor. (Courtesy Phillip Northman Collection.)

The old stone bridge, shown in the 1880s, provided passage across a stream and an entrance to the carriageways in the park, which were named for the primary cities in Georgia. The longest trail was named Savannah to honor the original British Colonial settlement and oldest city in the state. Others were named Americus, Augusta, Macon, Brunswick, Columbus, Rome, and Milledgeville. (Courtesy Phillip Northman Collection.)

A wooden footbridge led visitors to the lake and to the zoo. At the far end of the bridge, the sign above the arch points visitors to the Atlanta Cyclorama, where a painting depicting the Battle of Atlanta was open for viewing. The buildings that make up the zoo can be seen on the hill across the lake. In 1900, the city's 90,000 residents visited the park so frequently that the park hosted one million visits. (Courtesy Phillip Northman Collection.)

Atlanta, Ga.

Lake Abana was the centerpiece of Grant Park, providing recreation and relaxation to several generations. The boathouse, at the north end of the lake, provided visitors an opportunity to view the lake from the pavilion on top or rent a boat to row the calm waters. The lake survived into the 1960s, when it was drained to make way for parking and zoo expansion. (Courtesy Phillip Northman Collection.)

LAKE ABANA, GRANT PARK, ATLANTA, GA.

Postmarked 1908, this postcard is a photograph of Lake Abana with the boathouse in the center left. Swan Island can be seen in front and to the right of the boathouse. The six-acre, linear lake was created for storm water management; however, it also received water from numerous natural springs in and around the park. (Courtesy Phillip Northman Collection.)

16

The stone lion acted as sentry on Fort Walker. The fort is one of the last remaining remnants of defensive fortifications built to protect the city from the advance of General Sherman and his troops in 1863–1864. It is located in the southeast corner of the park. (Courtesy Phillip Northman Collection.)

Fort Walker became a very popular historical site and gathering place. In 1886, a letter from then governor Joseph Brown to park commissioner Sydney Root places several state-owned, Civil War–era cannons on loan to the city to be placed on Fort Walker. The cannons provided a backdrop for countless group photographs. (Courtesy Kenan Research Center at the Atlanta History Center.)

Fort Walker, Grant Park, Atlanta, Ga.

Col. Lemuel P. Grant was commissioned by the Confederate States of America (CSA) in 1863 to locate, design, and build defensive fortifications around the city. Colonel Grant planned for 20 redoubts placed strategically on the perimeter road approximately 1.25 miles from the center of the city. The fortifications were connected by trenches. This 1910 postcard shows cannons and a monument on the fort. (Courtesy Phillip Northman Collection.)

The defensive fortifications formed a 10.5-mile protective ring around the city and made it one of the most fortified cities in the world. Although the city did fall to Sherman's troops in September 1865, the fortifications forced Sherman to change tactics and slowed his advance. Fort Walker was positioned to protect the southeastern flank of the city. (Courtesy Georgia Archives, Vanishing Georgia Collection, FUL103.)

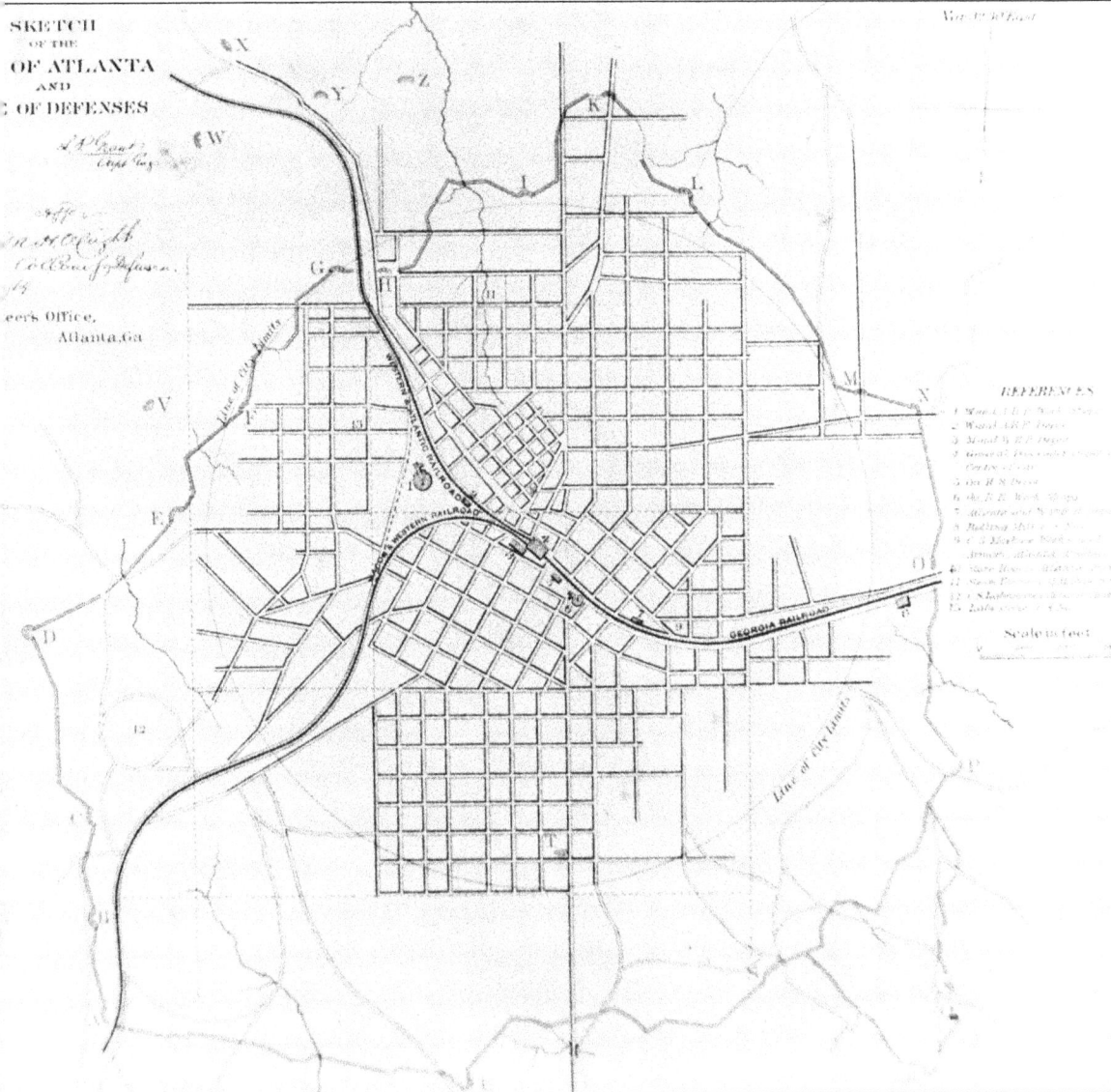

The line of defenses built around the city in 1863, under the supervision and design of L.P. Grant, are shown in this map. The city limits, which extended 1.25 miles from the center mile post, are indicated with a circle. The uneven line around the city indicates the placement of defenses. The construction was completed in about six months. (Courtesy Kenan Research Center at the Atlanta History Center.)

The fort was given its name after the war to honor Maj. Gen. W.H.T. Walker, "Shot Pouch" or "Fighting Billy" as he was known to his men. Walker, a native of Augusta and a West Point graduate, was shot and killed by a Union picket as he was reconnoitering enemy positions. Pictured, another generation visits the fort. (Courtesy Grant Park Neighborhood Association Archives.)

The monument pictured in this postcard honors Confederate general Walker and is placed on a spot near Leggett's Hill, about a mile east. There is a similar monument nearby that honors Union general James "Birdseye" McPherson, who was also killed during the battle. McPherson was the highest ranking Union officer killed in the Civil War. (Courtesy Phillip Northman Collection.)

It was not uncommon for veterans of both sides to commemorate the Battle of Atlanta. In 1886, the 35th Georgia Regiment assembled downtown, marched to Marietta Street, and boarded streetcars to Grant Park. Quoted in the *Atlanta Constitution* on September 25, 1886, a veteran from Dayton, Ohio, said, "This visit is a deal pleasanter than the one I made here 22 years ago. It's warm today, but gentlemen, let me tell you when I met the Georgia and Mississippi boys in gray out here on Peachtree Street it was uncomfortably warm." (Courtesy Georgia Archives, Vanishing Georgia Collection, FUL45.)

Close by the new park, the brick entry gates to Oakland Cemetery welcome visitors. The City Burial Place, or Atlanta Graveyard as it was first called, was established in 1850. It was renamed Oakland in 1872. The oldest public burial ground in the city was designed as a rural garden cemetery. (Courtesy Phillip Northman Collection.)

Located in Oakland Cemetery, the *Sleeping Lion* is a monument to the Confederacy and its fallen soldiers. The lion sleeps until the Confederacy rises. Nearby and on the grounds of the cemetery stood a two-story farmhouse that served as a field headquarters for Confederate commander John B. Hood during the Battle of Atlanta in 1864. (Courtesy Phillip Northman Collection.)

ENTRANCE TO GRANT PARK, ATLANTA, GA.

The American Panorama Company, Milwaukee, Wisconsin, was commissioned to create a painting of the Battle of Atlanta in 1885. German artisans came to Atlanta, sketched the landscape, and interviewed veterans and residents to gain perspective. They then produced the world's largest canvas painting. The painting toured several cities before being placed in storage. George Gress purchased the painting in 1893, and it was placed in Grant Park. (Courtesy Phillip Northman Collection.)

An Irishman, Robert Barker, created the first panorama in 1787. Soon, cycloramas were touring the cities of Europe and gained popularity in the United States. The Atlanta Cyclorama became a new attraction to the park with its panoramic painting and Civil War museum. It also solidified the park's prominence in the life of the city by adding more reason for a trip to the park. (Courtesy Special Collection and Archives, Georgia State University Library.)

Entrance to Grant Park, Atlanta, Ga.

The Battle of Atlanta painting premiered in Atlanta in 1892 in a wooden building at the corner of Edgewood and Piedmont Avenues. It was moved to Grant Park in 1893. In 1921, the painting was moved to a new fireproof building designed by Atlanta architect John Francis Downing. The building pictured was the first permanent structure for the painting of the Battle of Atlanta. Before motion pictures were introduced, the panorama, or cyclorama, was a very popular attraction for audiences across the United States and Europe. The large paintings of this genre depicted battle scenes, historical events, biblical stories, landscapes, and famous structures, and they all required specially constructed buildings for display. When moving pictures were introduced, interest and attendance at the hundreds of cycloramas declined, and as a result, most of the paintings are lost to time. About 30 are still known to exist worldwide. (Courtesy Phillip Northman Collection.)

Visitors to the Atlanta Cyclorama sit in theater-style chairs and listen to a narration of events of the Battle of Atlanta as the painting moves slowly around them. In this scene, Confederate and Union soldiers battle to gain strategic position around the Hurt House. The oil on canvas painting is the largest in the world at just over 15,000 square feet and 10,000 pounds. The debris in the foreground and the soldier with rifle (lower center left) are part of a diorama that was added in 1936 as a project of the Work Project Administration (WPA). The diorama gives the painting a three-dimensional appearance. (Both, courtesy Phillip Northman Collection.)

112- Cyclorama Building, Atlanta, Georgia

The *Texas*, a steam locomotive from the Great Locomotive Chase or Andrews Raid, is on display at the Atlanta Cyclorama. In 1862, a group of Union spies seized the locomotive *General* and raced north to rendezvous with a Union force. The intent was to destroy rail lines and disrupt communications between Atlanta and Chattanooga. Confederates pursued the *General* in another locomotive, the *Texas*. The chase ended with the capture of the Union spies, eight of whom were hanged in the area where Park Avenue and Memorial Drive intersect. The eight were the first recipients of the Congressional Medal of Honor, which was awarded posthumously. (Courtesy Phillip Northman Collection.)

This postcard from the mid-1920s shows the new Atlanta Cyclorama building (1921) in the background and an updated concession and boathouse. The northern tip of Lake Abana is visible to the right of the boathouse. As the city expanded, amenities in the park were improved to meet the demands of a growing population. Carriageways were paved to accommodate automobile traffic. (Courtesy Phillip Northman Collection.)

26

A portion of the park sits at the lowest point in a drainage basin of more than 300 acres. Included in the Olmsted design plan are stone streambeds to follow and direct the flow of water. The natural springs added to that flow. Pictured here is the area around Constitution Spring. All the water flowed south to Lake Abana. (Courtesy Kenan Research Center at the Atlanta History Center.)

The Lake, Grant Park, Atlanta, Ga.

Lake Abana was a man-made body sustained by storm water and the flow of natural springs. There were five cool-water and mineral-rich springs in the park. Water was conveyed to the lake via stone channels and creek beds. In 1903, a system of pipes was installed that diverted the flow of water underground. (Courtesy Phillip Northman Collection.)

ATLANTA, Ga. The Lake - Grant Park. *Atlanta is a fine place. The ... hasn't come out yet. We walked around ... through the business part of the city yesterday ...*

In the early years, people referred to the park as a resort because of its heavily wooded trails, cool springs, the lake, and gathering spaces. The waters of mineral-rich springs were believed to offer healing or medicinal qualities, and visitors drank, bathed, and bottled the water for cooking. The resort offered respite from the noisy, dusty streets of town. (Courtesy Phillip Northman Collection.)

The bandstand hosted regular musical concerts that attracted crowds and provided a leisurely afternoon in the shade of large trees. Brass bands, quartets, and choirs filled the park with music. The modern gazebo is built in similar style and is a place for picnics, birthday parties, and, of course, small intimate concerts on lazy summer afternoons. (Courtesy Kenan Research Center at the Atlanta History Center.)

L.P. Grant was delighted in the idea of a park with abundant water features and fountains, all sustained by the many natural springs. Pictured is Bethesda Spring around 1890. The sculpture of an angel looking down upon the spring was a gift to the city from park commissioner Sydney Root in memory of his wife, Mary (Clarke) Root. (Courtesy Kenan Research Center at the Atlanta History Center.)

In 1889, George Valentine Gress purchased, at auction, a bankrupt circus. He and his business partner, Charles Northen, were interested in the railcars carrying the animals and equipment. He also recognized the local curiosity about the animals. Gress donated the animals to the city to establish a public zoo. City fathers chose to place the zoo in Grant Park because of its popularity. (Courtesy Phillip Northman Collection.)

Visitors by the thousands came to view the exotic animals at the zoo. The collection consisted of one hyena, two silver lions, one black bear, one jaguar, one elk, two fawns, two African lionesses, three monkeys, two wild cats, one raccoon, one Mexican hog, one camel, and one dromedary. The collection was hugely expanded in the 1930s with a gift from Asa G. Candler Jr. of his private menagerie. (Courtesy Phillip Northman Collection.)

The zoo grounds were improved with the addition of colorful, blooming flowers and shrubs, and the public was encouraged to enjoy both the exotic animals and the gardens. The original footprint of the zoo was small and designed to be in harmony with the park. (Courtesy Phillip Northman Collection.)

VIEW IN GRANT PARK SHOWING SUNKEN GARDEN, ATLANTA, GA.

A rose garden enhances the visit to the zoo in the early 20th century. Established in 1889, the zoo is one of oldest operating zoos in the United States and is one of the oldest tourist attractions in Atlanta. Its collection has grown over the years to include birds, reptiles, large and small mammals, arachnids, and amphibians. (Courtesy Phillip Northman Collection.)

In the Victorian era, people held a strong curiosity and appreciation of nature and its offerings. Sydney Root, the first park commissioner, loved the natural features of the park and believed them to be restorative to the industrious people of Atlanta. This tranquil scene on Lake Abana around 1890 invites the visitor to reflect on the serene and natural beauty of the park. (Courtesy Kenan Research Center at the Atlanta History Center.)

Little Switzerland, later to be called White City after the Chicago Exposition of 1896, was an amusement park located off Confederate Avenue, just blocks from Grant Park. While Grant was a public park, Little Switzerland was private. According to the *Atlanta Constitution*, April 27, 1890, this park provided greater entertainment than other parks like Grant, Peter's, and Ponce de Leon. (Courtesy Kenan Research Center at the Atlanta History Center.)

White City Amusement Park, Atlanta, Ga.

According to the *Atlanta Constitution*, April 27, 1890, "During the past winter the owners of Little Switzerland have made great improvements; have in fact remodeled the grounds. They have built lakes, ten pin alleys, and located amusements of various kinds. It has a large dance hall, and in addition to this, they have an elegant dining room and serve the choicest luncheons." (Courtesy Phillip Northman Collection.)

Approach to White City, Atlanta, Ga.

The grounds of Little Switzerland included gardens, blooming flowers, and a lake for boating like that of Lake Abana in Grant Park. A visitor, quoted by the *Atlanta Constitution*, stated, "Oh, how beautiful! How gorgeously grand! I never knew there was such a lovely place about Atlanta!" The *Constitution* article concludes, "In fact, it seems to be the universal opinion of all who visit Little Switzerland." (Courtesy Phillip Northman Collection.)

Scene at White City, Atlanta, Ga.

In the mid-1890s, Little Switzerland came to be known as White City under the ownership and management of Charles Chosewood. Chosewood, a member of the Atlanta City Commission, lived on Confederate Avenue near his park. More amusements were added, including the recently introduced ride called a Ferris wheel. The Ferris wheel made its US debut at the Chicago Exposition in 1896. (Courtesy Phillip Northman Collection.)

Charles Chosewood remained on the Atlanta City Commission for over 30 years and, at the time, was the longest serving councilman. His family moved to a large house on the corner of Boulevard and Delmar Avenue. They were able to win the concession rights to various parks in the city, including Grant, and made a living selling popcorn, carbonated drinks, and candies. (Courtesy Kenan Research Center at the Atlanta History Center.)

With attractions like White City and Atlanta's oldest park, the Grant Park area proved a strong attraction for pleasure-seeking individuals and groups alike. They came to explore the park's pastoral beauty and to take keepsake photographs against the backdrop of its lush foliage. (Courtesy Georgia Archives, Vanishing Georgia Collection, FUL0974-85.)

Two

A City Embraces
its Park

After the land was donated in 1883, residents of the city of Atlanta, and beyond, needed no urging to flock to the park. The Metropolitan Street Railway Company established a streetcar service to Grant Park where Victorian-era visitors could find diversions of both art and nature.

Mother Nature offered five natural springs, Bethesda, Saloam, Constitution, Sulphur Spring, and one nameless, to lure visitors. One was infused with sulphur and iron, while the others were freestone with cold, clear water. The *Gate City* notes, "the springs are numerous and are all delightfully situated at the foot of some lovely sloping hill, or by the side of some beautiful walk, over which the boughs on the overhanging trees sway and swing in the breeze."

There was also statuary for visitors to gaze at as they walked the many paths and across the brick and stone bridges through the park. There were two bronze lions, an 11-foot-high bronze stag, and a sundial. Besides bicycling and walking, park visitors could partake of lawn tennis and croquet, listen to bands in the music stand, sit in the pavilions, and sip refreshments from the concession stand.

Over the years, Grant Park has been home to a number of unusual, fun, and once-in-a-lifetime happenings and events. These include reunions of Civil War veterans, a Singer sewing exhibition that was complete with a tightrope walk across Lake Abana, and, supposedly, an escaped panther sighting. It was later determined that it was not an escaped panther terrorizing visitors but a rather large tomcat. In more recent years, the Atlanta Jazz Festival made its home in Grant Park and one year featured band legend Miles Davis.

Grant Park has played host to people who stroll its grounds, bike its pathways, and enjoy picnics on the lawns and serves figuratively and literally as the centerpiece of a neighborhood that sits a one mile from downtown Atlanta and the Georgia State Capitol.

This postcard from 1913 features the latticed arbor of the waiting gate in Grant Park. The gate provided a pleasant entry point to welcome park visitors. It also served as a shaded and serene place to await the arrival of the streetcar. The simple, yet functional, design and materials gave a touch of elegance to the space. (Courtesy Phillip Northman Collection.)

The public comfort station and concession was designed by famed Atlanta architect Neal Reid of Hentz and Reid and built in the early 1900s. It was needed to accommodate the increasing number of visitors who flocked to the park for respite. This postcard rendering is from 1910. (Courtesy Phillip Northman Collection.)

The most visited walking trails offered seating areas for rest, relaxation, and people watching. Formally dressed, people donned their finest to be seen in the park and to socialize with friends and family. Grant Park was the social gathering place and premiere public space in the city well in to the 1950s. (Courtesy Georgia Archives, Vanishing Georgia Collection, FUL1054-91.)

One of the most popular strolling areas was around the edges of Lake Abana. The structure in this picture was an entryway to the park and offered a holding area for horses and carriages and refuge in case of inclement weather. Carriages also used this avenue to traverse the lake. (Courtesy Georgia Archives, Vanishing Georgia Collection, FUL1055-91.)

Grant Park has been the site of many events and gatherings. Here, a group of schoolchildren come together in the park to learn about and to celebrate Japanese culture around 1900. A growing city, self-proclaimed to be the "Gate City to the South," Atlanta always had ambitions to become one the world's next great cities. (Courtesy Kenan Research Center at the Atlanta History Center.)

The Olmsted firm placed great thought into each of its commissions. Plans were made for storm water management, appropriate planting, access, spatial relationships, active and passive areas, and differing experiences. One component within the overall approach and process called for the design to meet the fundamental social and psychological needs of the park visitor. The two men in this photograph sit beside Lake Abana and appear to be engaged in serious discussion. (Courtesy Georgia Archives, Vanishing Georgia Collection, FUL0104.)

A family posing while on an outing in Grant Park in 1908 provides a window into the proper dress and social norms of the early 20th century. Although a thriving residential neighborhood grew up around the park, also known as Grant Park, visitors came from all parts of the city, and beyond, to enjoy its many amenities. (Courtesy Georgia Archives, Vanishing Georgia Collection, FUL0952-85.)

This photograph of a warm summer day provides another view of the popular boathouse on Lake Abana, which, for many years, formed the centerpiece of Grant Park. It was one of the most photographed features of the park. The *Gate City* states, "At the boathouse, boats and refreshment stands are rented out by the year, and last year the net profits of the boats alone was fifteen hundred dollars." Because rowboats rented for the minimal fee of a dime, they were quite popular with families and young lovers alike. Rowing across the lake provided people with a panoramic view of the park, allowing boaters to have a different perspective of the abundant flora and fauna of the park. The lake was yet another way of incorporating the Olmsted philosophy of including pastoral places along with recreational opportunities in order to meet the physical and psychological needs of people with one park. (Courtesy Georgia Archives, Vanishing Georgia Collection, FUL102.)

Grant Park was, and continues to be, one of the top destinations for family reunions. This photograph captures a moment during the Grant family reunion around 1890. L.P. Grant died in January 1893 and is buried at Westview Cemetery with his first wife, Laura (died in 1875); his second wife, Jane (died in 1912); and Jane's first husband, James R. Crew (died in 1865). (Courtesy Kenan Research Center at the Atlanta History Center.)

The *Gate City* states the following: "In the center of the lake is a small island, built securely of rock and sand, and blooming richly in summer with blossoms of bright color. A small willow dips its slender fingers downward from the mound and adds a pretty effect to the scene." (Courtesy Georgia Archives, Vanishing Georgia Collection, FUL101.)

The *Gate City* explains that "on the lake there are eleven boats, each bearing the name of a flower, and these are used constantly by visitors who pay a nominal sum for the privilege of rowing on the water." The publication touted the attributes of a city on the move. (Courtesy Georgia Archives, Vanishing Georgia Collection, FUL1053-91.)

The John Charles Olmsted design for the park included walking trails, carriage trails, and passive-use areas. Also included were areas for more active recreation, including baseball fields, a bicycle track, lawn tennis, and croquet grounds. These areas were located in the northeast corner of the park. (Courtesy Georgia Archives, Vanishing Georgia Collection, FUL678.)

"Around the lawn is the bicycle track, which is a quarter of a mile long and which is said to be one of the finest in the South," states the *Gate City*, published in 1890. Although the track was made for cycling, it was also used for horse riding, as pictured above. (Courtesy Grant Park Neighborhood Association Archives.)

In the second decade of the 20th century, a portion of Lake Abana was set aside for a public swimming area. A cement floor was installed and a bathhouse constructed adjacent to the pool, and when it was complete, Grant Park boasted the largest cement-bottom pool in the Southeast. The pool was a favorite spot during Atlanta's hot summers. (Courtesy Phillip Northman Collection.)

Two young women pose in front of the public pool in the 1940s. The pool remained a popular gathering place until it was closed and drained in the early 1960s. Several reasons are cited for its removal, including expanded parking, zoo expansion, and desegregation of public facilities. Years later, the pool was replaced with an Olympic-sized pool. (Courtesy Georgia Archives, Vanishing Georgia Collection, FUL155.)

The skating rink and pavilion were located in a large concrete structure placed in the center of the park. The top floor was used for skating, cotillions, and a number of social events. The lower floor was used for large group picnics, company outings, and family reunions. It was perched on a hillside, so from the second floor, there was a view to other sections of the park. This 1914 postcard shows a relatively new building ready to serve visitors for many years. It was removed in the late 1980s and early 1990s during major renovations to the zoo and the cyclorama. (Courtesy Phillip Northman Collection.)

Horsecar service began in 1871 on the major thoroughfares in the city. Steam and electric streetcar service began in the 1880s. To better service southeast Atlanta, Lemuel Grant and others organized the Metropolitan Street Railroad in 1882. Two lines—Pryor Street and Park Line—brought city dwellers to the new park and to the budding residential area around it. There were a number of private competing trolley lines in the city, including the Atlanta Street Railway, Gate City Street Railroad, West End and Atlanta Street Railroad, and the Atlanta and Edgewood Street Railroad. (Courtesy Georgia Archives, Vanishing Georgia Collection, FUL5.)

The old wooden boathouse was replaced with a more modern structure in the 1940s, but the draw and charm of the lake remained. The new structure included an updated concession. Longtime residents still talk of boating on Lake Abana, budding romances, and first dates in the park. (Courtesy Kenan Research Center at the Atlanta History Center.)

A bust and monument to Thomas Talbot was placed in Grant Park as recognition of his role in founding the International Association of Machinists (IAM) union in 1888. The bust was dedicated in May 1948. Talbot worked as a machinist repairing trains. The shop was later known as the Southern Railway Locomotive Shop on Windsor Street. Today, the organization is known as the International Association of Machinists and Aerospace workers. (Courtesy Philip Cuthbertson.)

In 1948, over 1,500 members of the International Association of Machinists gathered in Atlanta to celebrate its 60th anniversary. The IAM was founded in Atlanta in 1888 by Thomas W. Talbot, who worked for a railroad repair shop. When a site was selected to honor Talbot, Grant Park was chosen due to its prominence and the common bond of the railroad. (Courtesy Georgia Archives, Vanishing Georgia Collection, FUL610.)

The Judge John Erskine Memorial Fountain was a gift to the city from Mrs. Willard P. Ward, daughter of Judge Erskine. As elaborate as a sculpture, the bronze bowl is set on a bed of white Georgia marble and is surrounded on three sides by a marble bench, which was engraved with the signs of the zodiac. The artist commissioned to design and install the Erskine fountain was J. Massey Rhind, a well-known sculptor of his time. His chosen theme, "Glorious Water," honored the early years of Judge Erskine's life when he was a British sailor and travelled around the globe. (Courtesy Phillip Northman Collection.)

The Erskine Fountain is one of many commissions completed by J. Massey Rhind during his career. His work includes a statue of Pres. William McKinley, a set of doors at Trinity Church in New York City, and numerous fountains, public monuments, and architectural sculptures. The fountain was moved to the Ormond Street entrance to Grant Park in 1912. (Courtesy Grant Park Neighborhood Association Archives.)

The fountain's namesake, Judge Erskine, was an Irish immigrant who came to Atlanta in 1855. He was appointed to the Federal District Court in Georgia by Pres. Andrew Johnson in 1865. He had the honor of having his name placed into nomination for the United States Supreme Court by Pres. Ulysses S. Grant in 1868. However, Judge Erskine opted to forgo relocating to Washington, DC, and decided to remain in Georgia. He stayed a part of the Federal District Court until 1882. (Courtesy Grant Park Neighborhood Association Archives.)

Installed in 1927, the fountain on Cherokee Avenue at Milledge Avenue is a one-of-a-kind structure. The granite block, brick, and terra-cotta tile fountain operated via city water, pressure, and gravity. When bowls on the front filled, the water drained to a pool on the opposite side. The water in that pool drained to a small creek that then flowed to Lake Abana. (Courtesy Philip Cuthbertson.)

Affixed to large stone entry gates leading to a plaza in front of the fountain, twin bronze plaques mark its installation and dedication. The plaques pay tribute to the mayor, the Park Committee, and architects. Recognized are Mayor I.N. Ragsdale, Park Committee chair John A. White, committee member Charles L. Chosewood, general manager of parks L.L. Wallis, and others. Architects of the fountains, Edwards and Sayward, also designed Roosevelt High School. (Courtesy Philip Cuthbertson.)

The lower fountain on the east elevation is accessed by a double flight of curving stairs. The fountain has an arched grotto made of granite block. A smaller arch is cut in the back wall of the grotto, and a pool stretches out beneath the grotto. The pool is bordered by a low granite wall. The water source for this lower fountain is through a single pipe that is connected to the upper fountain. The 40-foot granite-block wall of the east side of the fountain is an imposing feature. The drop in elevation combined with the thick stone wall dampen street noise and make for an ideal setting for weddings, intimate musical performances, outdoor theater, or church services. This beautiful Art Deco fountain sits silent while waiting for a restoration that will give it life once more. (Courtesy Philip Cuthbertson.)

Snow is always an event in Atlanta and an opportunity to capture well-known sites in uncommon circumstances. This series of photographs from the early 1920s provides a different perspective on the boathouse on Lake Abana, the old stone bridge, benches along a walking trail, and a group of children frolicking in the snow on Cherokee Avenue at Augusta Avenue. (Courtesy Kenan Research Center at the Atlanta History Center.)

A respite for the park comes in winter. The wooden benches lining the shore of Lake Abana, normally filled with visitors from the city in the warm weather months, sit empty and silent. The grounds get a cold weather reprieve from the throngs that visit in spring, summer, and fall. (Courtesy Kenan Research Center at the Atlanta History Center.)

These children pause from play long enough for this photograph to be taken on Cherokee Avenue at Augusta Avenue. Most likely, they are on their way to the park to take advantage of the hilly topography or to build a snowman. Longtime residents speak warmly about growing up in Grant Park and their time in the park. (Courtesy Kenan Research Center at the Atlanta History Center.)

The classic stone bridge was an entryway to the wooded walking and riding trails in the park. It provided passage over a creek for carriage traffic and park visitors. The bridge was in place in 1890. Made of granite, each end cap displayed the head of a roaring lion. Bronze urns held greenery along its sides, and the floor was made of brick. (Courtesy Kenan Research Center at the Atlanta History Center.)

In 1940, as then gubernatorial candidate Eugene Talmadge campaigned across the state, he made a stop in Grant Park and hosted a huge watermelon picnic. He was elected to three nonconcurrent terms and made runs for the US Senate but lost both efforts. (Courtesy Special Collection and Archives, Georgia State University Library.)

As horse-drawn carriages gave way to automobiles, the carriage trails in the park were paved. Cars were allowed to pass through and park along the roadways. As time passed and traffic increased, park advocates called for a return to pedestrian use. The roads still exist but are closed to pass-through traffic and parking. (Courtesy Special Collection and Archives, Georgia State University Library.)

The athletic fields provide a place for pick-up games or organized team sports. Grant Park was, and is, a popular destination for company teams and leagues. Lights were installed to accommodate night play, and the athletic fields were expanded to accommodate the growing need. Here, Trust Company Bank sponsored a men's baseball and women's softball team. (Courtesy Special Collection and Archives, Georgia State University Library.)

The Trust Company women's softball team is pictured here in this undated photograph. Recreational fields were a part of the original design and plan for Grant Park. The Olmsted design sought to find a balance between active use and more passive pursuits. (Courtesy Special Collection and Archives, Georgia State University Library.)

Another attraction for families visiting the park, a Dentzel Carousel, was added in the 1960s. The Dentzel Factory manufactured only two or three carousels per year, and the company supplied parks throughout the East and South. All of the animals were hand-carved out of poplar or basswood, and the carousels often had original oil paintings as well. The arrival of the Great Depression spelled the end to the factory in 1929. The Grant Park Dentzel Carousel had 52 whimsical hand-carved animals, a calliope band organ, and ornate gold-leaf benches. After years of operation, the carousel was removed in the 1980s and placed in storage, which was where it remained until the 1990s. The City of Chattanooga purchased the carousel, had it painstakingly restored, and placed it on the riverfront in Chattanooga, where it continues to be a huge draw for families. (Courtesy Kenan Research Center at the Atlanta History Center.)

Zoo Atlanta, still housed in Grant Park, has always been a draw for visitors from both near and far. Willie B., a silverback gorilla, was one of the star residents of Zoo Atlanta for more than 35 years. The gorilla was named for one of the city of Atlanta's most popular mayors, William B. Hartsfield—who was himself a childhood resident of Grant Park. Willie's early days were passed in a glass-enclosed, tile cage with a tire swing and television for entertainment. With a major facilities renovation in the mid-1980s, Willie B. had his first experience with the outside world and with other gorillas since his arrival in Atlanta in 1961. He was successfully reintroduced to gorilla society. Upon his death in 2000, he was survived by children, grandchildren, and great-grandchildren. A statue of Willie B. can be found on the grounds of Zoo Atlanta. This photograph was taken shortly after Willie B.'s arrival to Atlanta. (Courtesy Kenan Research Center at the Atlanta History Center.)

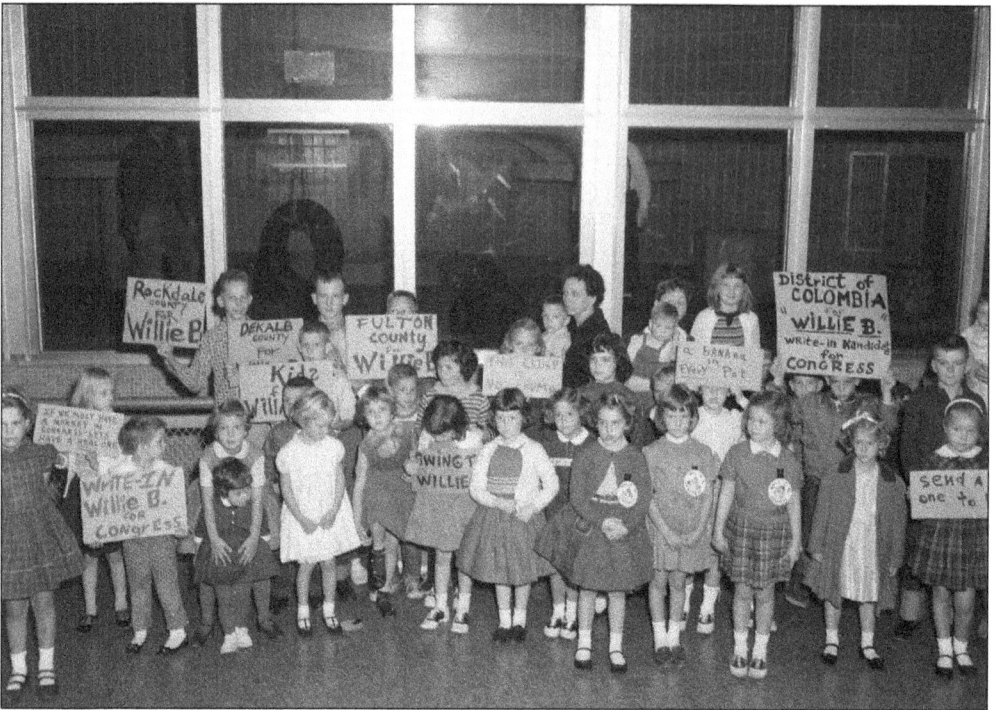

A group of schoolchildren campaigns for a write-in vote to elect Willie B, a silverback gorilla and zoo resident, to the US Congress. As the most prominent and most popular animal at the zoo during his 38-year stay, Willie captured the hearts of several generations of Atlantans. (Courtesy Special Collection and Archives, Georgia State University Library.)

A visitor is shown riding an elephant at the Grant Park Zoo. The municipal zoo operated for its first century under the purview of the City of Atlanta and Fulton County. Insufficient funding, poor management, and decreasing attendance led to a crisis, in which the facility was listed as one of the 10 worst zoos in the country. Its zoological certification was threatened. (Courtesy Kenan Research Center at the Atlanta History Center.)

This children's train was placed on the grounds of the zoo to provide added entertainment in the 1960s. A similar train continues to operate today and remains popular. With attractions like the zoo, the cyclorama, and the park itself, over two million visitors come to Grant Park each year. (Courtesy Kenan Research Center at the Atlanta History Center.)

Schoolchildren gather for lunch after visiting the zoo in this 1962 photograph. The animal enclosures can be seen in the background. It is a ritual that has lasted over 100 years, as thousands of children from across the state visit the zoo and the cyclorama each year. (Courtesy of Kenan Research Center at the Atlanta History Center.)

The Atlanta Cyclorama also contains a Civil War museum. Many of the artifacts and much of the memorabilia have been donated over the years. Pictured is a presentation and donation of a Confederate officer's uniform to be displayed in the museum. Tom Linder made the presentation. (Courtesy Special Collection and Archives, Georgia State University Library.)

Stars of *Gone With the Wind* Vivien Leigh (Scarlet O'Hara) and Olivia deHavilland (Melanie Hamilton Wilkes) visit the Atlanta Cyclorama in 1939. The film made its world premiere at the Loew's Grand Theater on Peachtree Street. Clark Gable was also on hand and asked to be included in the diorama. A Rhett Butler figure was added to accommodate his request. (Courtesy Special Collection and Archives, Georgia State University.)

In 1979, the Atlanta Cyclorama was closed for two years to undergo restoration to both building and painting at a cost of $14 million. Before this renovation, visitors walked through the painting. Now visitors are seated in a revolving theater that moves through each section of the painting. (Courtesy Georgia Archives, Vanishing Georgia Collection, FUL0153.)

The park was an inviting space for carriage rides or a ride on horseback. This undated photograph shows Minnie Bell Halsey (Mrs. Thomas R. Sawtel) posing on her mount. In most instances, the design of the park separated strolling pedestrian traffic from horse and carriage traffic. There were ample trails for both pursuits. (Courtesy Kenan Research Center at the Atlanta History Center.)

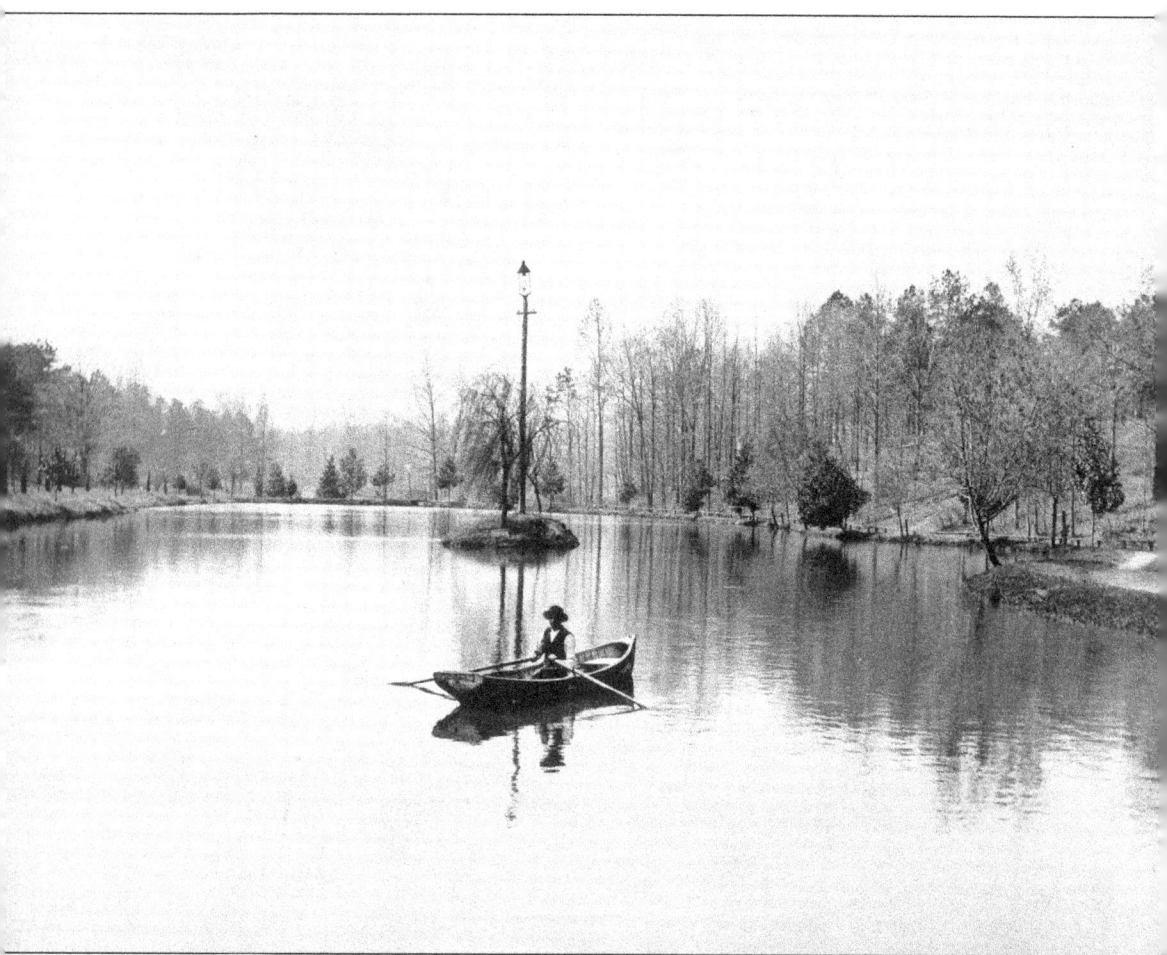

Lake Abana was not only an inviting place for recreation and reflection but also an anchor for the many features in the park, such as the Atlanta Cyclorama. A solitary boater rows quietly across Lake Abana in this 1895 photograph. A significant feature in this picture appears on the island directly behind the rower. An electric lantern towers over the island. While electricity was not new, it was still somewhat novel. In 1882, Thomas Edison's Pearl Street Power Station served about 85 customers and charged (in today's dollars) $5 per kilowatt-hour. The cost was significantly less in 1895. (Courtesy Kenan Research Center at the Atlanta History Center.)

Three

A Neighborhood
Grows up

Once Colonel Grant and other nearby property owners began selling off parcels of land, development of the Grant Park neighborhood occurred rapidly. Atlanta grew five-fold between 1865 and 1890, and Grant Park became an upper-middle-class neighborhood, populated with its first families in the 1890s. By 1893, almost all of the present-day roads were in place.

Around the turn of the 20th century, construction began in earnest. Large two-story mansions with front porches were built to face the park, while more modest homes populate the interior of the neighborhood. The first homes, constructed in the 1870s and 1880s, were in the Queen Anne and Folk Victorian styles.

The Queen Annes have steep-pitched, irregular rooflines and turned front porch supports with decorative spindle work. Some feature turrets. The Folk Victorian homes are mostly one-story cottages with gingerbread added to the porches and gables. Craftsman homes with gabled fronts and shotgun or double-shotgun houses were added to the housing mix in later years.

Commercial interests were also a part of the neighborhood, but rather than being concentrated in a central district, businesses were scattered throughout. Several grocery stores had salesmen who went out in horse and buggy to deliver orders to their customers. Besides grocers, the neighborhood had a drugstore with a soda fountain and a movie theater built in 1918 as a Masonic Lodge. Houses of worship and schools were also constructed to serve the growing number of families moving to Grant Park.

In 1857, Lemuel P. Grant built a home on today's St. Paul Avenue. It was situated on a high point on his 600 acres. He lived there with his first wife, Laura Williams (married 1843), and four children, John, Myra, Lemuel Jr., and Lettie. In a letter written to his wife in the late 1840s, Grant expresses his opinion that "this place will become a great city. Everything indicated that Atlanta would become a railroad center. It looked like a good place to stop and we stopped." Laura died in 1875 of pneumonia. Grant married Jane L. Killian Crew in 1881. She was a longtime widow of James R. Crew, a friend and associate of Grant. (Courtesy Special Collections and Archives, Georgia State University Library.)

Laura Loomis Williams was the daughter of Ammi Williams of Decatur. Her father was a native of Connecticut who was attracted to the area when he heard of a gold strike near Dahlonega, Georgia. He made his way to the Decatur area where he started a mill, which he later sold to Samuel A. Durand (1822–1891), and built a home, which he later sold to Benjamin Swanton. His real estate investments made him one of the largest landowners in the area. He owned much of the land that makes up downtown Atlanta today. Laura was fully engaged in social and civic pursuits. She helped raise funds to support Confederate troops during the Civil War and for veterans after the war. She died in 1875 of pneumonia.

Shortly after presenting his 100-acre gift to the City of Atlanta, Colonel Grant helped to ensure that a neighborhood grew up around it. He began to subdivide his property that bordered the soon-to-be park, and owners of nearby parcels did the same. The land was sold for residential development to Atlantans looking to live near the new park. The City of Atlanta also had an eye to its future and decided to expand its city limits and its tax base to ensure the bright future that Grant and others saw for it. They annexed most of the land around the park, which allowed them to take care of the sanitation and public safety needs of the residents of the new neighborhood. This map from 1902 details the new boundaries of the city of Atlanta. (Courtesy Michael and Carolyn Dufano Collection.)

The Grant Mansion was once a three-story home containing 8,200 square feet of living space. It had 20 rooms with 6 bedrooms, 9 fireplaces, 4 chimneys, twin parlors on either side of a central hallway, a ballroom, porches that wrapped around three sides, and hardwood floors throughout. This picture was taken in 1942. Unfortunately, the ravages of time, fire, and owners who have neglected it have left it a shell of a once grand home. The Grant Mansion has been the home of the Atlanta Preservation Center since 2001, when a potential buyer was looking to purchase the mansion in order to tear it down and build two new homes. It is one of the featured stops on the weekly walking tours that the center conducts in Grant Park, and the Atlanta Preservation Center plans to use it not only as their headquarters but also as a preservation resource center and a house museum. (Courtesy Kenan Research Center at the Atlanta History Center.)

In 1902, the Jones family from Canton, Georgia, came to live with Bryan Grant, a grandson of L.P., and his family in this home on St. Paul Avenue. Clara and Robert Jones were expecting their second baby and wanted to be near medical facilities. On March 17, family physician Dr. Kendrick delivered Robert "Bobby" Tyre Jones Jr. (pictured above) in the Grant's home. (Courtesy Kenan Research Center at the Atlanta History Center.)

Bobby Jones won golf's four major tournaments of the day in 1930. He is revered as one the best golfers in history and was involved in the creation of the Master's Tournament in Augusta, Georgia. The parade on Peachtree Street was in honor of his accomplishments on the links. Jones is buried in Oakland Cemetery, which is on the north edge of Grant Park. (Courtesy Kenan Research Center at the Atlanta History Center.)

In 1941, Margaret Mitchell, author of *Gone With the Wind*, loaned Boyd Taylor $3,750 to purchase the Grant Mansion and begin work on restoration. She believed it to be hugely important to the architectural history of the city and had hopes of restoring the house to be a living museum. In a partnership with Taylor as the live-in caretaker, Mitchell invested with high expectations. Unfortunately, the business relationship did not go well between Mitchell and Taylor. Mitchell was not satisfied with the progress or approach Taylor was taking in the restoration of the home. She filed a breach of contract suit in Fulton Superior Court and obtained a restraining order to prevent Taylor from removing anything from the property. In the end, Taylor retained ownership and occupancy of the home. Mitchell was killed when struck by a vehicle on Peachtree Street in 1949 and is buried in Oakland Cemetery. (Courtesy Kenan Research Center at the Atlanta History Center.)

Two separate fires destroyed the third story and then most of the second story of the house. It stood as a testament to neglect. A visual reminder of a city too busy to care, it was also a symbol for a surrounding neighborhood challenged by years of decline. In the 1990s, what remained of the second floor was removed for safety and insurance concerns. (Courtesy Atlanta Preservation Center.)

Through all its tribulations, the Grant Mansion still holds a number of original features. The window in a side parlor is framed by the original heart pine sills and casings. Open to the elements for years, matching parlors on either side of the grand hallway now have temporary protective roofs and new floors. A thoughtful and meticulous restoration is under way. (Courtesy Atlanta Preservation Center.)

Porches are the most common feature on homes in Grant Park. This mother and child enjoy a rocking chair on their porch on Hill Street. Porches provided an escape from the summer heat inside and became social gathering places. Because most homes were built close to the street, an evening stroll offered many opportunities to visit with neighbors. (Courtesy Kenan Research Center at the Atlanta History Center.)

Homes in the Grant Park neighborhood reflect a range of architectural styles. Queen Anne, Victorian, Craftsman Bungalow, New South Cottage, shotgun and double shotgun can be found, but what is more common is a home with characteristics from several recognized styles. Today, many of the homes sport yellow and blue sunbursts designed to reflect the flourishes found in the architecture and are a symbol of restoration efforts in the neighborhood. (Courtesy Kenan Research Center at the Atlanta History Center.)

71

There were a number of large grand homes built primarily around the periphery of the park and on the north and south avenues and streets. But the neighborhood has a mix of styles and sizes, as there were also many smaller homes built to accommodate the merchant and working class who moved to the neighborhood later. The increasing wealth of the area is reflected in the scene of a family on Hill Street photographed with their home and horse-drawn carriage (previous page). The large dining room of another neighborhood home is elaborately set for what looks to be a celebration. Elegant wood molding around the windows, like that in this dining room, and crown molding are common in homes throughout the neighborhood. (Above, courtesy of Georgia Archives, Vanishing Georgia Collection, FUL412; below, courtesy of Kenan Research Center at the Atlanta History Center.)

This house on Delmar Avenue is one of the oldest and largest with the most land in the Grant Park neighborhood. Built in 1868 by J.J. Williams as his country house, it is reported that he purchased the land from John Seals of DeKalb County, publisher of the *Sunny South* newspaper. The purchase price—22,000 Confederate notes. (Courtesy Marian and David Dye.)

William Tecumseh Montgomery and his wife, pictured with their granddaughters Helen and Frances, purchased their house in 1928. William's son James Andrew (J.A.) purchased the house from his parents in 1941. The house remained in the family until 1995, when J.A.'s daughter Marian and her husband, David, sold it to Bob Ward. (Courtesy Marian and David Dye.)

A young J.A. Montgomery agreed in 1941 to purchase the family home for $7,500 and to maintain it. The house was divided into four apartments, and J.A. lived in each one while he renovated and made repairs. As a paint contractor in the Depression era, making ends meet was always a challenge. He farmed his land and worked odd jobs in order to maintain his home. (Courtesy Marian and David Dye.)

The Montgomery family and home are pictured in 1930. A family member writes, "Her porch became a place to sit and share, love, cry, hope, and debate not only about our day, but the past and future. With additions to her walls, came additions to the family that was to live here for the next 70 years." (Courtesy Marian and David Dye.)

From left to right, Joyce, Holly, and Star, daughters of William Montgomery, pose in the side yard of their Delmar Avenue home. Over the years, the house has seen a handful of owners, including J.J. Williams, Laura Plumb (1879), Levisa Chamberlain (1900), E.H. Pitkins (1904), K.C. Williams (1906), J.C. Harvil (1927), the Montgomery family (1928–1995), and Bob Ward (1995 to the present). The 1934 plat for the Montgomery home indicates lots 8 and 10 Logan Plat Subdivision. The original street name was Logan. It was changed to Delmar Avenue after the turn of the 20th century. The property was originally part of Henry County, then DeKalb County, and finally Fulton County. Annexation to the city of Atlanta came in the early 1900s. (Both, courtesy Marian and David Dye.)

PLAT OF PROPERTY OF

WILLIAM T. MONTGOMERY

FOR

HOME OWNERS LOAN CORP.

LOTS 8 & 10 LOGAN PLAT SUBD.

LAND LOT 22   14TH DISTRICT

FULTON COUNTY   ATLANTA, GEORGIA

SCALE 1"= 60'   JUNE 29, 1934

J. W. BURPITT, C. E.

APPLICATION NO. 9-A-8081

The Fischer home on Boulevard was built in 1886 by Julias A. Fischer, a contractor and a purveyor of Fischer's New England Cough Bitters. A listing in the city directory of 1892 reads the following: "Fischer Bros. (Julias A. & Hartford C.) Contractors & Builder 164 Whitehall, Special attention given to repairing. Plans & estimates furnished on short notice. Telephone #898." In Julias Fischer's obituary (1934), he is said to have been one of the leading contractors in the city, a charter member of the Atlanta YMCA and its first secretary, a chairman of the Oakland Cemetery Board for eight years, a member of the City Water Board, a Knight Templar, a Scottish Rite Mason, a Shriner, and a member of Knights of Pythias and Atlanta Lodge of Elks No. 78. (Courtesy Tom Jennings and Tony Raffalovich.)

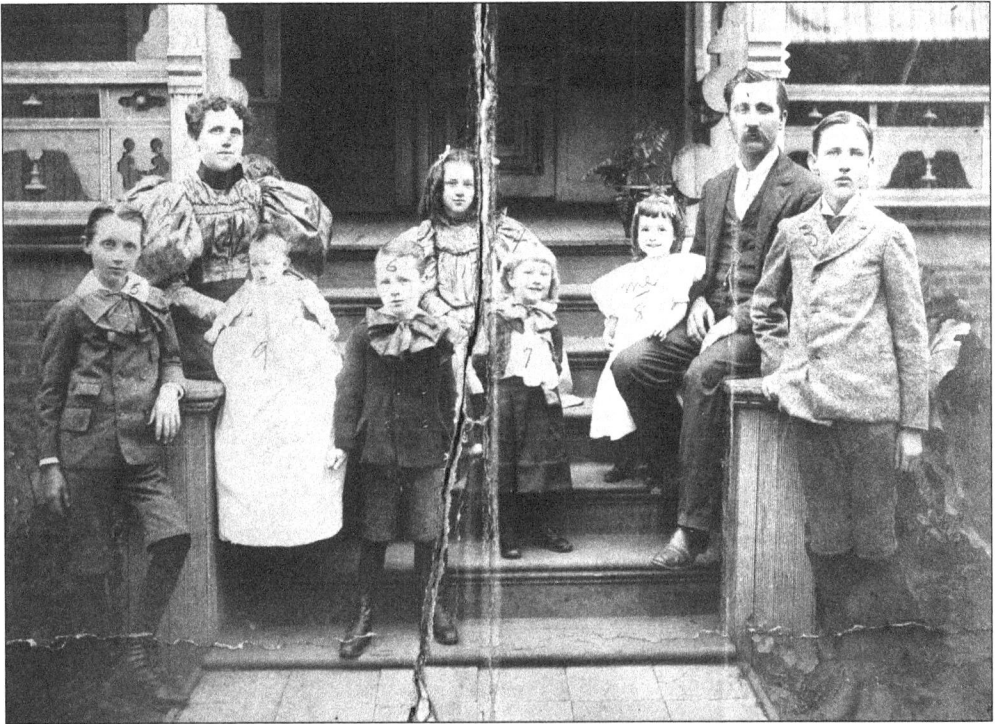

Julias Fischer and his wife, Georgia Belle, had 12 children, 2 of whom died in infancy. When the children had grown, the Fischers moved to what is now the Morningside area of Atlanta. The house, like many other large homes in the neighborhood, was subdivided in the 1920s. (Courtesy Tom Jennings and Tony Raffalovich.)

FISCHER'S
N. E.
COUGH BITTERS.

—FOR—

Coughs, Colds, Croup, Sore Throat, Hoarseness and Bronchial Troubles.

DOSE—Adult from one to two teaspoonfuls 3 times a day. During s___s of coughi'g a few drops additional can be taken to allay the symptoms.

Children in proportion to age.

There are persons who will receive more prompt relief by incre___ or diminishi___ regulation ___ as the nature o___ r cases demand.

THE FISCHER COUGH BITTERS CO.
PROPRIETORS.
Atlanta, Georgia.

The market was open to all kinds of concoctions and home remedies, touting the curative features of a product, regardless of effectiveness. Fischer sold his cough bitters to druggists across Atlanta. This label from a bottle found in the attic of the house gives dosage instructions for adults and children. (Courtesy Tom Jennings and Tony Raffalovich.)

James Enoch Jackson and his wife, Caroline Sumpter Rawlins Jackson, built a large house on their land at the corner of Atlanta and (South) Park Avenues in 1896. The surrounding acreage was subdivided and sold. It is still referred to as the Jackson O'Bryant Subdivision. Jackson family members lived in the home until 1971 when Jean and Neil Shorthouse and Bill and Jean Milliken purchased the house. (Courtesy Jean Shorthouse.)

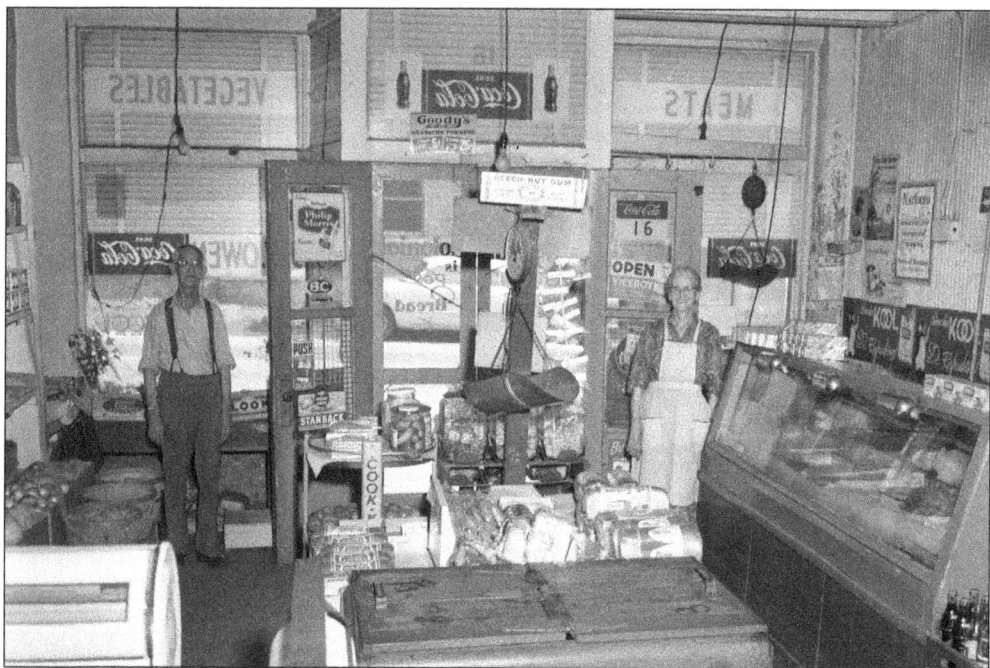

Because the neighborhood preceded the automobile, small grocers and dry goods stores opened in convenient locations throughout the area. Residents could walk or bike to purchase everyday items such as cheeses, meats, and even live chickens and pigs. Bell, Waters, Weinman, and Smithoff's Grocery were just a few of the merchants serving the area. Pictured is the E.H. Hendrick Grocery on Georgia Avenue. (Courtesy Special Collection and Archives, Georgia State University Library.)

Other nearby shops on Edgewood Avenue, Decatur Street, and in downtown Atlanta offered more specialized items such as clothing, furniture, and home items. This tobacconist shop, H. Silverman Company, was located on Edgewood Avenue, just blocks from its Grant Park neighbors. (Courtesy Georgia Archives, Vanishing Georgia Collection, FUL422.)

Before the automobile, many of the stores were not set up for customers to come in and shop. Rather, salesmen would go door-to-door taking orders and later would load up the store's horse and buggy and drive through the neighborhood delivering orders. It has been said the horses knew the routes so well that they led the way, allowing the shopkeeper to hand out orders to waiting customers. (Courtesy Georgia Archives, Vanishing Georgia Collection, FUL0136.)

Hyman Weinman, a Russian immigrant, opened this small grocery in 1914. He and his family lived in the attached house (left) and operated the store for many years. Over time and various owners, this store, most recently known as Kelly's Grocery, closed in 2003. The Kelly family purchased the store in 1974 and also lived in the attached house. Doris Kelly then sold the operation in 1995. She received a lifetime lease on the house for $1 a year and remained there until her death. It was the longest, continuously operated grocery in the city, but like so many of the small shops in the neighborhood, it fell victim to large grocery chains and the convenience of the automobile. (Courtesy Jones/Ellas Design Collection.)

Along with the automobile came auto accidents. This two car pile-up at the corner of Woodward Avenue and Grant Street quickly drew a crowd of onlookers and disrupted customer traffic at the A.S. Byatt Market (background). The people in the windows above the store lived in apartments on the second floor. (Courtesy Special Collections and Archives, Georgia State University Library.)

Beginning in the 1870s, trolleys were introduced to Atlanta. The first were horse or mule drawn. Steam and electric streetcars were introduced in 1880. There were a number of competing private companies serving the area. In 1902, all lines were consolidated into the Georgia Railway and Power Company (now the Georgia Power Company). Five separate trolley lines served Grant Park. (Courtesy Georgia Archives, Vanishing Georgia Collection, FUL0733-83.)

Fire Station No. 10 was located on Boulevard, north of its present location. This turn-of-the-century photograph shows the modern firefighting equipment and the firehouse in the background. Most of the structures in the area were built of wood. In 1917, a major fire destroyed 2,000 buildings and left 10,000 residents displaced. The fire began just blocks north of the Grant Park neighborhood and raced north, sparing Grant Park from its ravages. (Courtesy Georgia Archives, Vanishing Georgia Collection, FUL076-83.)

On its way to the scene of an emergency, this fire truck from Station No. 10 lost control and swerved into a commercial building on Memorial Drive. The old horse-drawn wagons were outdated and had given way to more modern vehicles in an effort to reduce response times. (Courtesy Georgia Archives, Vanishing Georgia Collection, FUL0844083.)

In 1907, St. Paul United Methodist Church moved to its new sanctuary on Grant Street. The congregation began on Easter Sunday 1867 when members of Trinity Methodist Episcopal Church South held a mission service at a Fair Street hospital for Civil War veterans and their families. The hospital was unable to hold all the people. The mission grew, and by 1870, St. Paul Methodist Episcopal South was opened on Hunter Street with 63 members. (Courtesy St. Paul United Methodist Church Archives.)

Before the official opening of its new granite-block Neo-Romanesque building, members gathered in the sanctuary for this photograph. The next step in construction would include the installation of carved wooden pews, an organ, choir loft, pulpit, and altar. The floors are heart pine and remain in the church today. (Courtesy St. Paul United Methodist Church Archives.)

Highly detailed stained glass windows depicting the Crucifixion of Jesus Christ and other biblical scenes wrap the sanctuary in warm natural light and are a reflection of a growing congregation, its wealth, and commitment to the church. This photograph features one of the large windows on the south-facing wall of the sanctuary. (Courtesy St. Paul United Methodist Church Archives.)

By 1921, St. Paul boasted more than 2,300 members and was the largest Methodist congregation in the Southeast. The church continued to grow and hold a prominent place among churches in Atlanta for decades. After World War II ended and families moved from the city to more suburban locations, the church began to lose membership. The trend continued into the 1970s. (Courtesy St. Paul United Methodist Church Archives.)

The pipe organ, now refurbished and still in use, was made by the W.H. Reisner Manufacturing Company, Inc., of Hagerstown, Maryland. The organ was part of an exhibit during the Cotton States Exposition in 1887. At the close of the exposition, the company did not want to go to the expense of shipping the organ back to the factory, so it was offered for sale. (Courtesy St. Paul United Methodist Church Archives.)

Just to the southeast of the Grant Park neighborhood is the Burns Cottage, an exact replica of the cottage where poet Robert Burns was born in Scotland. The Burns Club of Atlanta, established in 1896, began plans for the cottage in 1907. It was completed in 1911 and has been used for club meetings since that time. (Courtesy Atlanta History Center.)

The growing residential area attracted families with children. Schools became an important part of the community and included Slaton, Jerome Jones, and Fair Street Elementary Schools and Girls High to name a few. This group of schoolchildren posed for a picture around 1911 at a school, possibly Jerome Jones School, on Home Avenue, a block east of Boulevard. (Courtesy Kenan Research Center at the Atlanta History Center.)

Fair Street School was located between Grant Park and downtown and served the neighborhood's growing elementary school population. Renamed Memorial Drive, Fair Street was a busy thoroughfare even back then in the corridor, located between Grant Park and downtown. Fair Street had several trolley lines that ran along it. (Courtesy Kenan Research Center at the Atlanta History Center.)

Girls High was the only all-girl school at the time it was established in 1872 along with Boys High and five elementary schools. The 104-room Neo-Byzantine building housing Girls High was constructed in 1924. Designed by the architectural firm of Edwards & Sayward, Girls High continued serving an all-female student body until 1947. (Courtesy Georgia Archives, Vanishing Georgia Collection, FUL0420.)

The dome in this photograph is a striking architectural feature and is constructed of copper set on a circular drum of alternating arched windows on square pillars, which appear as brown and white bands. In 1937, a cafeteria and boiler house were added to the facility, funded through the Work Progress Administration. A gymnasium was added in 1950. The building was converted to apartments between 1986 and 1988. (Courtesy Kenan Research Center at the Atlanta History Center.)

As national elections approached in 1932, candidate Franklin Delano Roosevelt (FDR) made a campaign stop in Atlanta. His motorcade took him through Grant Park and through the campus of Girls High. He campaigned for a "New Deal" for the millions suffering the effects of the Great Depression. With 57.4 percent of the popular vote and 472 electoral votes, FDR went on to defeat Herbert Hoover in the November election. FDR's administration created the Works Progress Administration, the Public Works Administration, the Federal Emergency Relief Administration, and many other initiatives to bring jobs and prosperity. Roosevelt died at his Little White House in Warm Springs, Georgia, in 1945. (Courtesy Kenan Research Center at the Atlanta History Center.)

In 1947, Girls High went coeducational, and for the first time, both female and male students attended the school. In that year of change, and in honor of the late President Roosevelt, the school was renamed Roosevelt High School. When the school was converted to apartments, the new owners retained the name Roosevelt. (Courtesy Kenan Research Center at the Atlanta History Center.)

Girls High transitioned to a coeducational facility with a new name in 1947. Roosevelt High School was one of two high schools to serve Grant Park after Hoke Smith Middle School converted to a high school. The rivalry between the two schools was intense—one representing the east side of the neighborhood, while the other was on the west side. (Courtesy Special Collection and Archives, Georgia State University Library.)

In 1875, Amos Giles Rhodes came to Atlanta as part of L&N Railroad. He started a small furniture business and went on to become a wealthy merchant and leading citizen. In 1904, a new home for the Atlanta Circle of the King's Daughter and Sons, a hospital for patients with incurable diseases, opened on Church Street (now Carnegie Way). Desperate to make needed repairs to the building, hospital officials asked Rhodes for money to repair the roof. Rhodes responded by giving enough money to purchase land and construct a new building. Known today as the A.G. Rhodes Home, the building opened in 1904 at the corner of Woodward Avenue at Boulevard in Grant Park. (Courtesy Kenan Research Center at the Atlanta History Center.)

The Fulton Bag & Cotton Mill, located just north of Grant Park, was built in 1881. The business partnership between Jacob Elsas and Isaac May began as the Fulton Cotton Spinning Company. The mill manufactured paper and cloth bags. As the business grew, buildings were added to the complex in 1882, 1895, and 1907. (Courtesy Kenan Research Center at the Atlanta History Center.)

Elsas and May ended their business partnership in 1889, and Elsas incorporated as the Fulton Bag & Cotton Mill. The mill expanded, and a mill town was built around the facility. Labor strikes occurred in 1885, 1897, and 1914, and demands included admittance to the United Textile Workers Union, better wages, a 54-hour work week, and reduction in child labor. The 1914 strike lasted into the following year but failed. (Courtesy Georgia Archives, Vanishing Georgia Collection, FUL0682-82.)

Grant Park Lodge No. 604 was chartered by the Most Worshipful Grand Lodge of Georgia in October 1918. Initially, the group met at St. Paul Church on Grant Street and then in a storefront on Grant Street at Glenwood. Within five years of establishing the lodge, membership grew to 330, and a building was erected on Cherokee Avenue at Glenwood at a cost of $52,000. (Courtesy Philip Cuthbertson.)

On the second floor of Lodge No. 604, there was a banquet hall that hosted many official celebrations for Grant Park Lodge members and Masons from across the city. Pictured is the Eastern Star installation of Ruby Adams, who lived on Rosalia Avenue. The banquet hall now sits empty, but it is mostly intact. (Courtesy Special Collections and Archive, Georgia State University.)

In 1934, the Grant Park Temple Theater opened to packed houses each night. Cinema was a new and growing industry, and the Masonic Lodge Building was retrofitted to accommodate the theater. At the same time, the grand movie houses, Fox, Loew's Grand, and Rialto, were opening downtown. The Temple Theater remained in operation for three decades. (Courtesy Special Collection and Archives, Georgia State University Library.)

A group of adults decided to open a Sunday school to benefit the many children in the city in 1870. Many adults were attracted as well, and "Preaching Services" were added to the weekly schedule. On December 24, 1871, a mission was organized in the name of the fifth Baptist church of Atlanta in a building on Bell and Gilmer Streets. (Courtesy Park Avenue Baptist Church Archives.)

The congregation outgrew the space and moved to a new building at the corner of Cherokee and Woodward Avenues in Grant Park in 1901. The congregation purchased a lot at the corner of Park Avenue and Sydney Street for a new facility, and in 1932, ground was broken for a new Sunday school building. The sanctuary was built in 1938. (Courtesy Park Avenue Baptist Church Archives.)

Glen Castle, currently operating as a transitional housing facility, began as the Atlanta Stockade, or the Atlanta City Jail. The land was purchased in 1863 for a public cemetery; however, it was used for other purposes, and in 1896, the jail opened on the property. The building visible today was constructed in 1904. Following a new trend, the building was of concrete construction. It is one of the oldest concrete buildings in the city. (Courtesy Philip Cuthbertson.)

16671

In 1889, Henry W. Grady of the *Atlanta Constitution* began a Soldiers' Home initiative with an editorial in the paper. Many veterans of the Civil War were homeless, destitute, or living in poor houses. Grady called upon the people of Atlanta and Georgia to raise the dollars necessary to build a home for "these men who gave so much." The building was erected at a cost of $45,000 and then given to the state with the condition that the state appropriate funds for the cost of operations and maintenance. Governor Atkinson would not accept the added cost to the state. It was not until 1899 that the state legislature allocated $15,000 per year for care and maintenance. The home could then be opened and occupied. (Courtesy Kenan Research Center at the Atlanta History Center.)

The original wooden structure burned in September 1901. The Atlanta Fire Department did what they could to save the building, but it was beyond the city water limits. Fortunately, there were no injuries. As soon as temporary housing was arranged for the residents, an effort was organized to replace the home. A new Soldiers' Home opened in 1902. (Courtesy Kenan Research Center at the Atlanta History Center.)

As the home aged and its mission to Confederate veterans faded, the Soldiers' Home was demolished. The State of Georgia built a new facility on the land where the home once stood. Erected in 1956, the headquarters for the Georgia State Patrol still makes its home at this facility along with several other state agencies, including the Georgia Emergency Management Agency, Department of Transportation Office of Traffic Management, the Office of Homeland Security, and others. (Courtesy Special Collection and Archives, Georgia State University Library.)

The Federal Penitentiary is a mile south of Grant Park. Completed in 1902, the 300-acre complex was built to accommodate up to 1,200 inmates. It was designed by the architectural firm of Eames and Young of St. Louis, Missouri, the same company that designed the Leavenworth facility. Some of the better-known residents to be held in Atlanta include Al Capone, John Gotti, Vincent Papa (French Connection), Bernard Madoff, Carlo Ponzi, and Socialist Party candidate for the presidential election of 1920—Eugene Debs. He received over 900,000 votes while incarcerated. In the 1980s, hundreds of Mariel Boatlift refugees not eligible to remain in the United States were held in Atlanta. When the United States negotiated a repatriation agreement with Cuba, refugees, not wanting to return to Cuba, rioted and took control of a large section of the facility, causing extensive damage. The facility is now a transfer unit for prisoners moving from one prison to another. It also houses medium and minimum security inmates. (Courtesy Kenan Research Center at the Atlanta History Center.)

With a large neighborhood now encompassing it, the park continued to be a draw for families. In 1955, these two unidentified girls visited Grant Park and enjoyed the view from Lake Abana. They were among the last generation to be able to walk along this feature, as it was demolished in the 1960s. Gone now are the lake and the largest cement-bottom pool in the Southeast. An outdoor Olympic-sized pool now serves the area in a different location in the park, and a small pond, also in a different location than Abana, provides a water feature in the park. (Courtesy Kenan Research Center at the Atlanta History Center.)

Four

A NEIGHBORHOOD
IN TRANSITION

In later years, the automobile shaped Grant Park for better and for worse. The neighborhood was split in half in the 1950s to make way for Interstate 20. Many Victorian-era homes, as well as the James L. Key Golf Course, were demolished. This, and a general exodus from the city to the suburbs, led to many home owners moving out of the neighborhood and caused many of the local businesses to decline as well.

When many of the once great homes in the neighborhood were subdivided, they became boardinghouses and multifamily apartment houses. This caused the fabric and the atmosphere of the neighborhood to change. It lost its Victorian-era charm and became a more transient neighborhood with a declining number of owner-occupied homes. Crime rates soared, earning the neighborhood the reputation of being crime riddled, unsafe, and undesirable. In fact, at one time, it had one of the highest crime rates in the city of Atlanta.

Fortunately, the 1970s brought a few people back to the neighborhood who wanted to purchase the vintage homes and restore them to their former glory. Because this trickle of people turned to a flood in the 1980s, 1990s, and into the 2000s, Grant Park has seen a revival. The sound of hammering and sawing frequently competes with the songs of the still plentiful birds.

New homes have been added to the mix of the old, and most have been built keeping with the designs of the original ones. The neighborhood has adopted the sunburst as its symbol, and many houses have one hanging on their front porch. The designation as a historic district helps ensure that the fabric and feel of the neighborhood will remain the same. Zoo Atlanta, the cyclorama, and the park itself bring visitors to the neighborhood year-round. New and noteworthy eateries bring Atlanta diners to the neighborhood night after night.

This series of four photographs provides a glimpse of a quiet residential area in the 1948–1954 range. The intersection of Woodward and Oakland Avenues (facing east) shows a corner shop, sidewalks, a mature tree canopy, and street parking. Most of the homes in Grant Park were built before people owned automobiles. There were few driveways and even fewer garages. (Courtesy Special Collection and Archives, Georgia State University Library.)

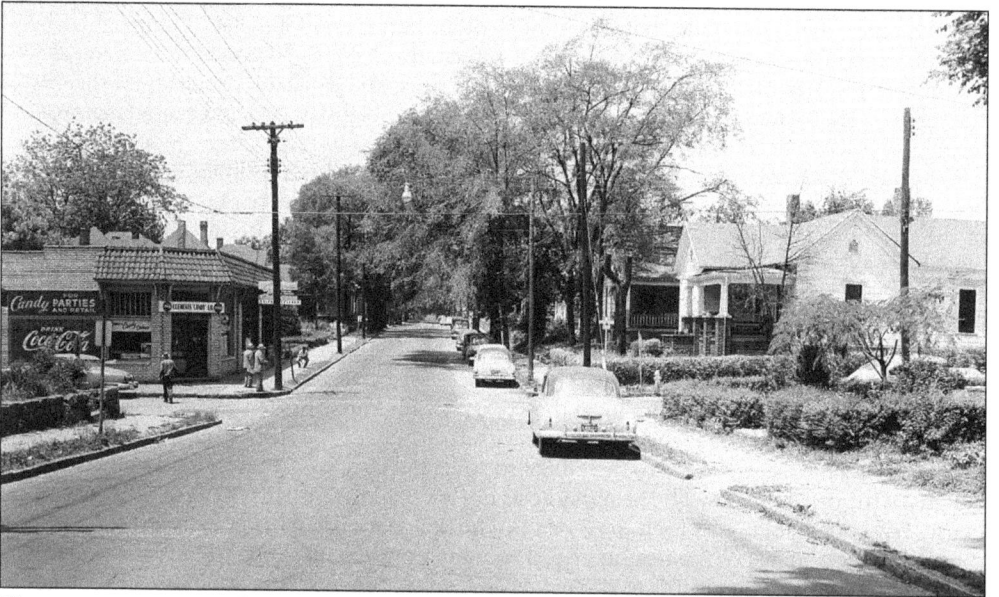

The same intersection, facing west, is shown in this photograph. This tranquil scene gives no clue of the coming disruption to the area when interstate highway construction will move through. Corner shops like these were scattered throughout the neighborhood and provided gathering places and shopping. Many of these commercial nodes still exist, but some of the buildings have been converted to new uses. (Courtesy Special Collection and Archives, Georgia State University Library.)

The intersection of Woodward and Oakland Avenues facing north looks toward the brick wall of Oakland Cemetery, across Memorial Drive. The homes on the right side of the street are no longer in existence, and most of the land where they once stood is now commercial property. (Courtesy Special Collection and Archives, Georgia State University Library.)

The southern view of the same intersection shows Oakland Avenue continuing south to where it stops at Cherokee Place. Construction of Interstate 20 in the 1960s and 1970s changed this perspective dramatically. Today, this photograph would depict a highway sound and visual mitigation wall just two blocks beyond the intersection. (Courtesy Special Collection and Archives, Georgia State University Library.)

By the beginning of the 20th century, Atlanta was the regional rail hub of the Southeast. The vision L.P. Grant had as a new resident in the 1840s became a reality. Rail was the driving force in shipping of goods, travel, and industrial growth. Union Station, first built in 1854, was destroyed by Union forces in 1864. The station was rebuilt in 1871. This 1908 photograph shows a crowd welcoming the introduction of new passenger rail service to the city. Passengers could travel to most cities across the country from Atlanta via rail. (Courtesy Kenan Research Center at the Atlanta History Center.)

In 1930, a new Union Station was constructed. It was the smaller of two rail passenger stations serving the city and was a reaffirmation of the importance of rail to the economy of Atlanta. The last passenger train departed from Union Station in April 1971. In the next year, it was demolished and replaced with parking lots. In 2010, there is new discussion of passenger rail service revolving mostly around commuter service and high-speed rail between cities like Savannah, Chattanooga, Charlotte, and Birmingham. (Courtesy Kenan Research Center at the Atlanta History Center.)

Terminal Station, built in 1905, was the largest passenger rail station in Atlanta. Designed by architect P. Thornton Marye of Washington, DC, the building featured twin Italianate towers and provided an imposing statement on the importance of the railroads. It was built by Atlanta contractors Gude & Walker. On the horizon, however, the increasing number of automobiles and a fledgling air transport business would provide passengers with more travel options. While passenger service would remain popular for decades, the introduction of interstate highways and air travel would eventually prove to be tough competition for passenger train services. Terminal Station, home of the Atlanta-to-Savannah *Nancy Hanks*, Atlanta-to-Washington *Southern*, and Atlanta-to-New Orleans *Crescent*, closed and was demolished in 1970. The Richard Russell Federal Building now sits where the grand rail station stood. (Courtesy Kenan Research Center at the Atlanta History Center.)

Aerial photographs from 500 feet above ground show a neighborhood intact in 1954. A maturing residential area with tree-lined streets, sidewalks, aging homes, and a connecting grid of roadways was in the direct sight line of progress. The ball field in the lower portion of the photograph is the northern tip of the park. At the top of the picture, Oakland Cemetery is visible with Memorial Drive bordering its southern edge. As transportation planners developed a route for a new interstate highway, the consequences for Grant Park and neighborhoods like it across the nation were yet to be understood. (Courtesy Georgia Department of Transportation.)

This 1974 aerial view, taken from 1,000 feet above ground, shows the division of the neighborhood by four lanes of high-speed traffic. In this picture, the ball fields in the lower right are at the northern edge of the park. Oakland Cemetery is again visible in the top-right corner. Hundreds of homes, a golf course, and residential streets were lost. In Grant Park, Rawson Street was completely removed, as were parts of Clarke Street. Cross streets, such as Grant, Oakland, Broyles, Cameron, and Chastain, were cut into north and south sections. The interchanges shown are Boulevard on the right and Hill Street on the left. The Hill Street interchange has since been reconfigured. (Courtesy Georgia Department of Transportation.)

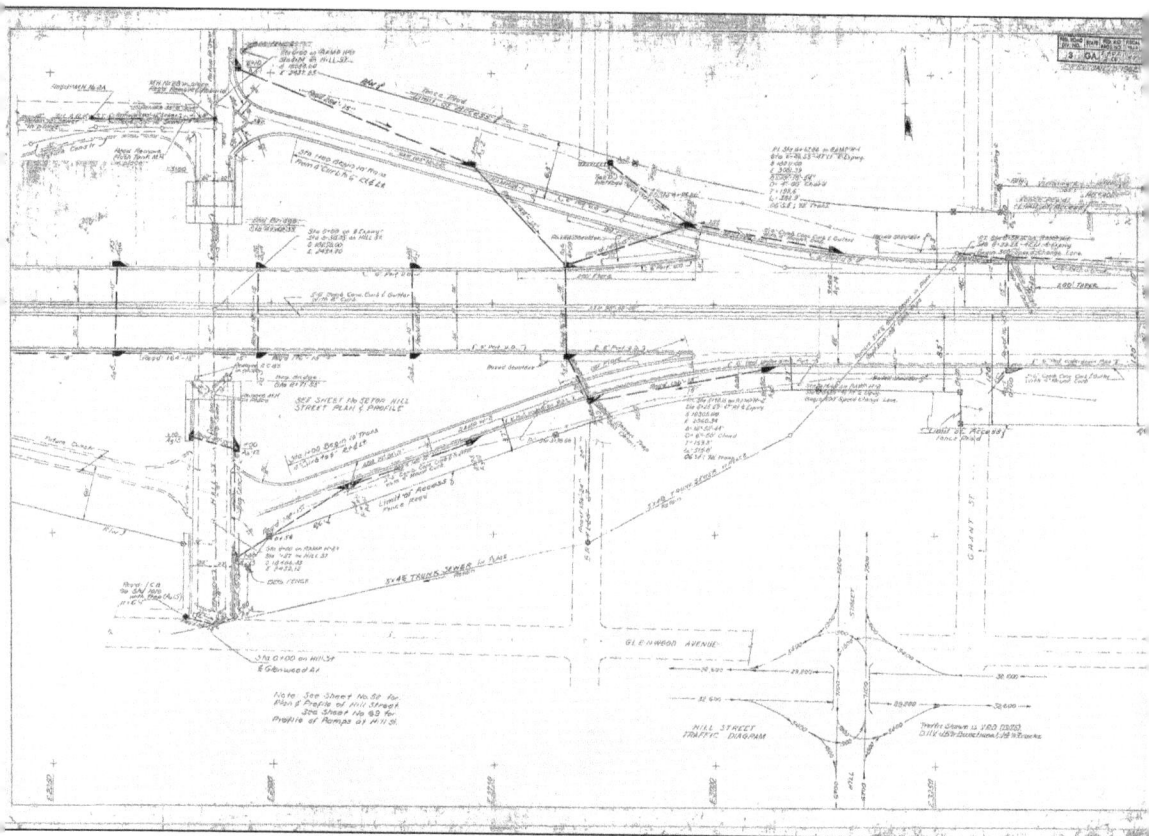

After World War II, Atlanta began another period of booming growth. Automobile traffic was increasing, and planning began for an interstate highway system to link cities across the country. Engineers and surveyors photographed, sited, and drew possible routes for Interstate 20 to move through Atlanta. This sketch shows an interchange between Grant Street and Capitol Avenue. Today, federal and state regulations require a much greater level of review and documentation before such projects can move forward. The Office of Environmental Services within the Department of Transportation is in charge of documenting the impact on historical and cultural resources, while working to minimize those impacts. (Courtesy Georgia Department of Transportation.)

The Memorial Drive corridor was a vibrant area filled with stores, small businesses, and light industry. This photograph shows the intersection of Grant Street and Memorial facing north. The neighborhood streets were laid out in a grid pattern, which has all the streets running south to north and east to west. (Courtesy Special Collections and Archives, Georgia State University.)

This view of Memorial Drive at Grant Street looking west on Memorial Drive includes the above-the-street electric lines for the bus trolleys. The rail lines for the old steam and electric trolleys remain beneath the paved surface of many streets, including Memorial Drive. (Courtesy Special Collections and Archives, Georgia State University.)

Grant Street makes a slight jog when it intersects Memorial Drive, and this view of the intersection is from Grant Street looking south. Memorial Drive lost most of its vitality after the construction of interstate highways and remained in a state of decline for decades. Its fortunes seem to be turning with the revitalization of the area in recent years. New restaurants, low-rise condominiums, and apartments have given the corridor new life. A new park is planned that will provide a linear green space between the Georgia State Capitol and Oakland Cemetery. Zoning guidelines limit building height and density to reduce any impact to homes in the area. (Courtesy Special Collections and Archives, Georgia State University.)

The construction of interstate highways impacted city neighborhoods all over the country. Grant Park suffered a slice right through its heart, as progress and growth brought a four-lane federal highway project through the area. The gaping cut created a physical and mental divide in the neighborhood. (Courtesy Special Collections and Archives, Georgia State University.)

The footprint of Interstate 20 is evident in this picture, as construction moves through this unidentified section of town, which is believed to be just west of Grant Park. The interstate was designed to move people easily through towns across the United States and caused Grant Park residents to move on to other areas of town. (Courtesy Georgia Department of Transportation, Office of Environmental Services.)

Downtown Atlanta, as viewed from the southwest in the area of Mechnicsville around the mid-1960s, shows the path of Interstate 20 and the intersection with Interstates 75 and 85. The Grant Park neighborhood is just blocks to the right (east). Grant Park has Interstates 75 and 85 running a mile to the west, and Interstate 20 also runs through it. (Courtesy Georgia Department of Transportation, Office of Environmental Services.)

Construction of a bridge at Capitol Avenue, located in the area where Interstates 20, 75, and 85 intersect, is pictured in 1960s. The gold dome of the Georgia State Capitol Building and the tower of Atlanta City Hall are in the background and within a short distance of Grant Park. (Courtesy Georgia Department of Transportation, Office of Environmental Services.)

110

Boulevard and Glenwood Avenues are shown here and both were forever altered by Interstate 20. Because of a major interchange and overpass, Boulevard is a heavily traveled thoroughfare that takes visitors from Interstate 20 to the zoo, the cyclorama, and the park. The corner building, Nabors Automatic Laundry, is long gone from the neighborhood. (Courtesy Special Collections and Archives, Georgia State University Library.)

Looking northwest on Boulevard from Sydney Street, this 1940s photograph reflects a quieter time when the neighborhood was still connected and the sounds of traffic were more muted. Today, if someone were to stand in this same spot, they would see the interchange for Interstate 20 just beyond the storefront in the left of the picture. (Courtesy Special Collections and Archives, Georgia State University Library.)

A later expansion of the Interstate 20 corridor created a six-to-eight-lane thoroughfare. Neighborhood activists and historical preservationists from Atlanta and nationwide advocated for a more balanced approach to major public works like highways. New laws and guidelines have been set in place to allow for broader impact studies, documentation of historical structures, and environmental impact reviews. While today's residents are resolved to having an interstate as a neighbor, they still battle the effects of noise, air quality, and the vast cut that divides the area from its once connected streets. (Courtesy Georgia Department of Transportation, Office of Environmental Services.)

By the mid-1960s, the neighborhood was moving rapidly into decline. The construction of the interstates exacerbated, and perhaps hastened, the trends already well entrenched. White families were fleeing to suburban locales where homes were new, schools were perceived to be better, and shopping and subdivisions offered a different lifestyle. Homes in Grant Park were rented or abandoned. (Courtesy Kenan Research Center at the Atlanta History Center.)

Many homes sat vacant, fell into disrepair, and became easy prey for thieves. Taken were some of the architectural gems left from the original construction, doors, mantels, light fixtures, and more. The downward spiral intensified, and the park followed suit. The grounds, like this yard, were poorly maintained, and the infrastructure crumbled. (Courtesy Kenen Research Center at the Atlanta History Center.)

What remained of the once numerous and thriving stores, like this one at Cherokee and Augusta Avenues, began to close. Urban blight paid a visit to Grant Park. While many of its residents continued to flee to the suburbs, a core of longtime residents did remain in the neighborhood. (Courtesy Special Collection and Archives, Georgia State University Library.)

Longtime residents speak of the overwhelming problems encountered during the downturn. They were determined to patiently and systematically address the most sever issues. Homeowners banded together to create a credit union to loan money for purchase and repairs, and another group of neighbors worked on crime issues. (Courtesy Special Collection and Archives, Georgia State University Library.)

By the mid-1970s, a few "urban pioneers" began to buy and live in homes in Grant Park. Values and pricing were well below other areas of the city. The housing stock was rich with history and solidly constructed. The turn started very slowly as bank loans for the purchase and/or renovation of homes were nonexistent. The area was written off by banks and other lenders due to "high risk." Residents banded together to raise the profile of the area and change perceptions. In the early 1980s, neighbors organized a tour of homes. It focused on active renovation and began to draw the curious. Organizers of the home tour added a party, appropriately called "The MothBall," designed to bring neighbors together and to build a sense of community. New trends also came into play—higher gas prices, desire for shorter commutes, and a movement back to cities. (Courtesy Kenan Research Center at the Atlanta History Center.)

Pictured is Hill Street looking south through the intersection with Georgia Avenue. A house now sits where the grocery once was. The house on the right looks as it did when this picture was taken between the 1940s and 1950s. After years of turmoil and decline, many Grant Park homes have been restored. (Courtesy Special Collection and Archives, Georgia State University Library.)

Looking east on Georgia Avenue from Hill Street, the park is a few short blocks away, and Georgia Avenue ends there. Originally, the carriageways in the park were named for the primary cities around the state, including Savannah, Augusta, Americus, Milledgeville, Brunswick, Rome, and others. (Courtesy Special Collection and Archives, Georgia State University Library.)

Confederate Avenue Baptist Church reflects the boom, bust, and resurgence of the Grant Park area. Once a thriving congregation, the church suffered from the flight of residents from the neighborhood. A small group tried to keep the church alive, but the doors closed, and the membership merged with Park Avenue Baptist Church. The building was vacant until the Vision Church of Atlanta filled the space in 2010. (Courtesy Philip Cuthbertson.)

This wedding photograph speaks to the vitality of Confederate Avenue Baptist Church in the mid-1930s. Unlike a number of churches that left the neighborhood and followed their membership to the suburbs, the Confederate Avenue church remained. Unable to draw new members, the church closed its doors and joined with Park Avenue Baptist Church. A new church body occupies more than 28,000 square feet of worship, office, and classroom space. (Courtesy Special Collection and Archives, Georgia State University Library.)

L.P. Grant married Jane Killian Crew in 1881. He had been a widower since 1875. Jane Crew was widowed in 1865. Grant decided to build a new home and began construction three blocks to the west of Grant Mansion, located on what is now the southwest corner of Hill and Sydney Streets. Grant sold his first house to his son. (Courtesy Philip Cuthbertson.)

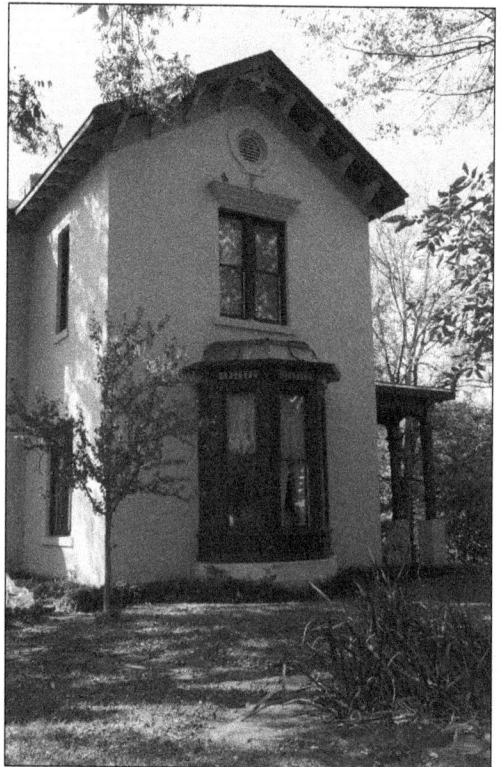

The second home of Lemuel P. Grant, now called the Grant Manor, was a large two-story home where Lemuel and Jane Grant lived until the 1890s. The house has wooden detailing in its eave brackets, porch posts with segmental arches, and two half-hexagonal windows. The manor is still in need of a makeover to restore its features. (Courtesy Philip Cuthbertson.)

The mid-1970s marked the beginnings of a turnaround for Grant Park. Urban pioneers purchased homes for remarkably small amounts of money and then placed the money they saved purchasing the house into restoration and renovation. During this time, blue tarp roofing was a main feature of many homes. Over the next few decades, the neighborhood transformed into a vibrant residential area. (Courtesy Philip Cuthbertson.)

Smaller homes in the neighborhood were simple with any architectural flourishes of gingerbread focused on the front of the house. Porches are also a main feature of the older homes. This house was built on speculation by Empire State Investment Company in 1906. An auction notice from September 1906 offers this house and 15 others and states, "The finishings are in clear Georgia pine. The mantels are handsome and appropriate great taste having been displayed in their selection." (Courtesy Philip Cuthbertson.)

The Burns home is another shining example of the active restoration of the older homes in Grant Park. It is reported, although not documented, that the house was once a high-class bordello. It is known that for many years it was a boardinghouse with 12 apartments. Painstaking restoration began in 1977. (Courtesy Philip Cuthbertson.)

The Burns Mansion ((1865–1868) was built and owned by James A. Burns. Burns was a Union officer involved in the Battle of Atlanta and, at the war's conclusion, remained in the area. The Queen Anne–style turret and masonry were a later addition to the house. Currently, the 8,000-square-foot house is one of the largest in Grant Park. (Courtesy Philip Cuthbertson.)

The old cobblestone streets are now paved with asphalt, but large sections of the original redbrick sidewalks are still in use. Historical guidelines now in place require brick or octagonal stone sidewalks to be replaced with like materials after construction projects. The Grant Park area was placed on the National Register of Historic Places in 1979. (Courtesy Philip Cuthbertson.)

The neighborhood design included a north-to-south and east-to-west street grid, homes built close to the front of properties, narrow deep lots, and alleyways behind homes. The alleys were for sanitation purposes, and many are still visible and used for rear access and parking. It is the responsibility of contingent property owners to maintain the alleys. (Courtesy Philip Cuthbertson.)

Directly across Grant Street from the Burns Mansion is a second Burns home. This large two-story was a gift from Captain Burns to his son on the occasion of his wedding. This home has also been expertly renovated in the last decade. Exterior renovation to the homes is monitored and regulated in order to protect the integrity of the structures. (Courtesy Philip Cuthbertson.)

The Grant Park neighborhood submitted an application to the city in 1999 for designation as a historic district. A group of individuals dedicated thousands of hours to document the homes and buildings in the area and develop preservation guidelines. With more than 1,400 contributing structures, Grant Park is now the largest historic district in the city. (Courtesy Philip Cuthbertson.)

An important component of a vibrant community, schools moved to the forefront as more families moved to Grant Park in the 1990s. For years, as children reached school age, parents moved to the suburbs. However, some stayed and worked to improve the schools. With steady improvements and high levels of parental involvement, schools in the area have seen great improvements. Families now seek out the neighborhood based on the performance in its schools. Parkside Elementary, located on land the White City Amusement park once occupied, is part of the City of Atlanta School District. (Courtesy Philip Cuthbertson.)

Slaton Elementary School on Grant and Pavilion Streets opened in 1907. It was named for William Martin Slaton, longtime principal at Boys High and then superintendent of Atlanta Schools from 1907 to 1915. The building now houses the Neighborhood Charter School, which has become a popular alternative for many families. (Courtesy Philip Cuthbertson.)

Local architect Eugene C. Wachendorff designed Slaton Elementary. He is also credited with the designs of Crawford Long Hospital and Booker T. Washington High School. The building was cleaned and painted in preparation for the new Charter School in 2002 only to be gutted by fire the following year. It was rebuilt and reopened in 2005. (Courtesy Philip Cuthbertson.)

Water's Grocery closed decades ago and sat vacant for years. The building has found a new purpose as office lofts. Small shops and commercial buildings are found throughout the neighborhood. With the resurgence in the area, many of these shops are finding new life in the old structures. (Courtesy Philip Cuthbertson.)

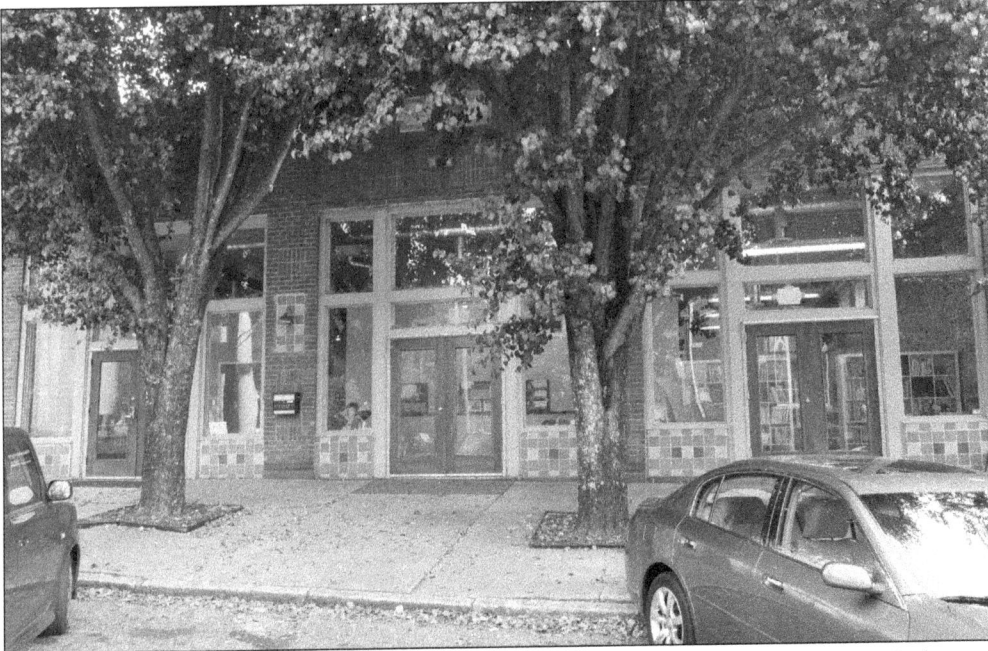

The Chosewood Building on Georgia Avenue at Grant Street is another example of adaptive reuse of space. Over the years, the building has operated as an A&P grocery, a health clinic, a thrift store, and most recently as offices. Owners have taken an interest in saving and preserving old structures while putting them to new use. (Courtesy Philip Cuthbertson.)

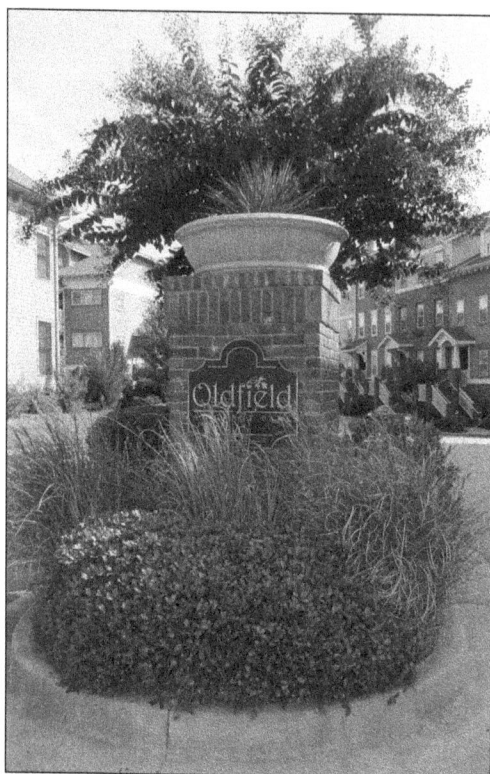

During the building boom of the 1990s and 2000s, new developments came to Grant Park offering condominiums, single-family homes, and apartments. Oldfield is a condominium and townhouse complex on the southeastern edge of the neighborhood. Developers shied away from the area for decades. As plans are developed for new construction and infill housing, builders are encouraged to blend into the architectural fabric under historic guidelines. (Courtesy Philip Cuthbertson.)

The Enclave, a townhouse and detached single-family home development, replaced an old industrial site occupied for decades by Superior Rigging. The influx of new residents has attracted new restaurants and shops in an area around Memorial Drive. These are all more signs of the turnaround, as developers showed little interest in Grant Park not too long ago. (Courtesy Philip Cuthbertson.)

Since 1883, there has been one constant in the area—the park. Grant Park has been, and continues to be, one of those pieces of city life that provides a sense of place and uniqueness. Gone are the private homes lining Peachtree Street, the steam and electric trolleys, Rich's and Davison's Department Stores, and many other icons of the city that made Atlanta, Atlanta. Fortunately, places like Grant Park remain to anchor the city in its past and to welcome its future. Even Lake Abana is only a fond memory held by many older Atlantans. This photograph, taken in the last years of the lake's existence, is a reflective view of the concession and boathouse. (Courtesy Kenan Research Center at the Atlanta History Center.)

Sydney Root (1824–1897) held great respect and love for nature. Although L.P. Grant had considered making a gift of land to the city for years, Root convinced his friend the time was right to do so. When the land was gifted to the city in 1883, Mayor John B. Goodwin appointed Root as the first park commissioner. It became his responsibility to oversee the development and beautification of the resort at Grant Park. L.P. Grant loved to walk through the woods on his property, to listen to birds, to enjoy the trees, and to hear the gurgling springs. Since that time, millions of visitors have been given the same experience because of the vision and generosity of Lemuel Pratt Grant. (Courtesy Kenan Research Center at the Atlanta History Center.)

Visit us at
arcadiapublishing.com